SpringerBriefs in Economics

For further volumes:
http://www.springer.com/series/8876

Carol Yeh-Yun Lin · Leif Edvinsson
Jeffrey Chen · Tord Beding

National Intellectual Capital and the Financial Crisis in Bulgaria, Czech Republic, Hungary, Romania, and Poland

Springer

Carol Yeh-Yun Lin
Department of Business Administration
National Chengchi University
Taipei
Taiwan

Leif Edvinsson
Universal Networking Intellectual Capital
Norrtälje
Sweden

Jeffrey Chen
Accenture
Chicago, IL
USA

Tord Beding
TC-Growth AB
Karlstad
Sweden

ISSN 2191-5504 ISSN 2191-5512 (electronic)
ISBN 978-1-4614-8017-4 ISBN 978-1-4614-8018-1 (eBook)
DOI 10.1007/978-1-4614-8018-1
Springer New York Heidelberg Dordrecht London

Library of Congress Control Number: 2013940444

Printed on acid-free paper

Springer is part of Springer Science+Business Media (www.springer.com)

Foreword I

The economic crisis is a consequence of many parallel factors which are all related to globalization and digitalization. My main concern, assessing this in more detail from the European perspective, is that revolutionary global forces have not been taken early nor seriously enough by most national and regional decision makers. The Heads of European States and Governments have once again recalled the importance of fiscal consolidation, structural reform, and targeted investment to put Europe back on the path of smart, sustainable, and inclusive growth. The main question is how capable and ready are the national governments to tackling the complex and manifold issues of crises and to renewing even radically many of our public and private structures and processes.

The first basic requirement is that all the European Union Member States remain fully committed to taking the actions required at the national level to achieve the objectives of the Europe 2020 Strategy. The second basic requirement is that the national and regional governments, as well as people, are ready for radical changes. This booklet, and the other 11 booklets by the experienced authors, focus on National intellectual capital (NIC) and give necessary insights and facts for us the readers and especially for our in-depth systemic thinking of the interrelationships of NIC and economic recovery.

How should the national and regional decision makers tackle the existing knowledge of intangible capital? The focus needs to be more on the bottom-up approach stressing the developments on local and regional levels. I highlight our recent statements by the EU Committee of the Regions. The key priorities are to get more innovations out of research and to encourage mindset change towards open innovation.

The political decision makers are finally aware that the traditional indicators created for and used in industrial production cannot be applied to a knowledge-intensive, turbulent, and innovativeness-based global enterprise environment. Indicators that perceive the intangible dimensions of competitiveness—knowledge capital, innovation knowledge, and anticipation of the future—have been developed around the world, but their use has not yet become established in practice. This booklet accelerates the development and the use of these indicators.

This helps the local and regional, as well as central, governments in taking brave leaps forward on a practical level—giving greater ownership and involving all the stakeholders. This means the need of actions towards increasing the structural and relational capital of regions, both internally in communities of practice and in collaboration with others.

The new generation innovation activities are socially motivated, open, and collectively participated, complex and global by nature. The regions need to move towards open innovation, within a human-centered vision of partnerships between public and private sector actors, with universities playing a crucial role.

Regions should be encouraged to develop regional innovation platforms, which act as demand-based service centres and promote the use of international knowledge to implement the Europe 2020 Strategy, smart specialization and European partnerships according to the interests and needs of regions. For this to happen, we need to apply the new dynamic understanding of regional innovation ecosystems, in which companies, cities, and universities as well as other public and private sector actors (the "Triple Helix") learn to work together in new and creative ways to fully harness their innovative potential.

New innovative practices do not come about by themselves. One major potential is the use of public procurement. The renewing of the European wide rules must increase the strategic agility and activities of municipalities and other public operators as creators of new solutions. Especially, the execution of pre-commercial procurement should be reinforced even more in combination with open innovation to speed up the green knowledge society development, i.e., for common re-usable solutions in creating the infrastructures and services modern real-world innovation ecosystems are built upon. Conditions must be created that also allow for extensive development projects which address complex societal challenges and which take the form of risk-taking consortia.

One of our working instruments within the Committee of the Regions is the Europe 2020 Monitoring Platform, which broadly reviews and reflects the opinions and decisions on regional level all around Europe. It gives a flavor of cultural and other socioeconomic differences inside the EU. This brings an important perspective to the intellectual capital, namely the values and attitudes needed for citizens supporting policymakers on appropriate long-term investments and policies.

Emphasizing the importance of these issues, decision makers in all countries and regions worldwide need a deep and broad understanding of the critical success factors affecting the NIC. With all the facts and frames for thinking this booklet gives a valuable insight in today's challenges.

Markku Markkula
Advisor to the Aalto University Presidents
Member of the EU Committee of the Regions
Former Member of the Parliament of Finland

Foreword II

Financial crisis—words very much heard today. What is all this about, actually, and how to get a grip on what we experience today? The booklet gives an important insight on the factors affecting competitiveness and productivity in modern knowledge society. We need to see behind the obvious, and we need to have increasingly "qualified guesses" as the character of the society and industry has fundamentally changed.

What is very important to notice is the shift towards intangible value creation beyond the deterministic phenomena we saw very clearly in the industrial era. Cost drivers were the important ones throughout the industry. Mass production, bigger is better; very traditional productivity factors, was the mantra.

However, the production picture is changing. Increasingly value is created by the intangibles, often services related to the tangible components, and even totally in immaterial value creation, where perceptions and expectations determine the market value of the "extended product". We also see rapid change in organizational forms, we see new type of entrepreneurship growing besides the traditional industry clusters, we see smart specialization of regions and countries.

This means also that there will be clearly different and complementary roles of the actors in innovation and value creation ecosystems. Large companies, small ones and even microenterprises together with the public sector are traditionally seen as the active partners in such innovation environments. The real issue in the dynamic markets is, however, that the end users are increasingly to be taken on board as *active subjects* for innovation, and not merely treated as objects, customers. Markets need to be shaped and created in much more dynamic way than ever before. Open innovation beyond cross-licensing includes the societal capital as an important intangible engine for productivity growth. Innovation happens only when the offering is meeting the demand. Otherwise, we can only speak about inventions or ideas.

We need to have a close look at the intellectual capital and the different factors within it when we design our policy approaches. Short-term investments in process capital (infrastructures) and market capital seem to be very important for the manufacturing base as such, but at the same time measures for longer term intellectual capital development and efficiency need to be taken.

Increasingly, important is the *structure* and the open *processes* related to intangible capital and knowledge pools. For sustainable long-term development both the *human capital and renewal capital are crucial*, as they are directly related to the innovation capability of the region. The correlation between these factors and the GDP growth is undisputable. In knowledge intense industries talent is attracting talent, and the connectivity which modern ICT provides makes this talent pool fluid across disciplines, organizations, and geographical settings. It is imperative to modernize the innovation systems enabling the full dynamics needed for success in knowledge intense industries, beyond the traditional boundaries.

Measuring performance of innovation systems becomes increasingly complex due to the mash-up of different disciplines, having new types of actors and interactions between them. Hence, the importance of analysis of the various components of the national intellectual capital (NIC) (and equally on national innovation capability) as done in this booklet cannot be underestimated when making qualified guesses for operational choices to create functioning innovation ecosystems. The only predictable in true innovation is the unpredictability and the surprises. The role of the public sector is to drive strategy and measures enabling the unpredictable, and to catalyze a fluid, seamless and frictionless innovation system to grow, with strong interplay with the surrounding society.

We need to have courage to experiment, to prototype in real-world settings, to have all stakeholders involved to find and remove the friction points of innovation and to achieve sustainable innovation ecosystems for knowledge-intensive products and services.

I wish you interesting reading with this mind opening report.

Bror Salmelin
Advisor, Innovation Systems
European Commission
DG CONNECT

Foreword III

The 2008 global financial crisis hit the whole world with unprecedented speed, causing widespread financial panic. Consumer confidence dropped to the lowest level since the Great Depression. Taiwan, with an export-dependent economy, was seriously impacted by the crisis and the unemployment rate hiked while household consumption levels dropped. At the onset of the financial crisis, Prof. Lin was the Dean of Student Affairs here at National Chengchi University in Taipei, Taiwan. She was the dean in charge of financial aid and student loans and thus saw firsthand the direct impact the financial crisis had upon our students. The crisis was so devastating that Prof. Lin, along with the university, was compelled to launch several new initiatives to raise money and help students weather the difficult times.

I am very glad that she took this painful experience to heart and set herself upon the task of investigating the impact of the crisis; trying to look into the causes and consequences for policy implications, not only for Taiwan but for an array of 48 countries. In particular, she approaches the crisis from the perspective of "national intellectual capital (NIC)" which is very important in today's knowledge-driven economy.

Taiwan is an example of a knowledge economy and has enjoyed the fame of being referred to as a "high-tech island". Without an abundance of natural resources, Taiwan's hardworking and highly educated population is the single most precious resource that the island has. Acknowledging the value of such human resources and intellectual capital, we established the Taiwan Intellectual Capital Research Center (TICRC) under my leadership in 2003. Ever since then, Taiwan's government has continuously funded the university to conduct relevant research projects aimed at enhancing the intellectual capital of Taiwan. Having been thus endowed with the responsibility of nourishing future leaders in the public and private sectors, we have focused on building up our strength in innovation, entrepreneurship, and technology management related research and education.

To enhance intellectual capital research, we recently formed a joint team of professors for a 4-year project in order to leverage their respective research capabilities. Through this project we hope to provide policy suggestions for the government by exploring the creativity, innovation, and intellectual capital at national, regional, city, and county levels. The goal is to come up with an intangible assets (IA) agenda for Taiwan's future sustainability. Professor Lin is an integral member in this research team.

Following her 2011 book *National Intellectual Capital: A Comparison of 40 Countries*, this booklet series is Prof. Lin's second attempt at presenting her research, conducted under the sponsorship of TICRC, to international readers. As the Founding Director of TICRC and her President, I am honored to give a brief introduction of the value of this booklet series.

In comparison to her 2011 book, this series increased the number of countries studied to 48 and particularly focuses on the impact of intellectual capital on the 2008 global financial crisis. Rarely has an economic issue been systematically studied from the view point of IA, particularly at such a large scale of 48 countries. The research results show without a doubt that NIC is indeed an important economic development enhancer. In particular, the fact that countries with higher NIC experienced faster recoveries from the 2008 financial crisis provides a strong message for the policymakers.

In addition to providing insights to national policy, the booklet also summarizes the background of each country before the crisis, the key events during the crisis, economic development afterwards, and future prospects and challenges. Each volume affords readers a holistic picture of what happened in each country in an efficient manner. The linkage between NIC and this financial crisis also provides a different perspective of the crisis.

We are happy that Prof. Lin continues to share her valuable research results with international readers. I sincerely hope that her insights can garner more attention concerning the benefits of developing NIC for the well-being of every nation.

Se-Hwa Wu
Professor, Graduate Institute of Technology
and Innovation Management
President, National Chengchi University
Taipei, Taiwan

Preface I

There are "mounting risks of a breakup of the Euro zone." Such comments are frequent today on how the European leaders are handling the escalating crisis and its potential impact on non-European countries. But few leaders, reporters, or researchers are actually addressing the situation of national intellectual capital (NIC) and its signals. In addition to the financial crisis, is there an emerging NIC crisis as well? Why is it emerging? How should policymakers think about NIC? In what way does it need specific attention? When will the outcome and impact of taken NIC policy steps be realized?

In the midst of the European crisis, there are national interventions to address the issues mentioned above. In leading economical nations the investments going into intangibles now exceeds tangibles, and is positively correlated to income per capita. However, these still do not show up clearly in national mapping as well as policy making insights. Therefore, the New Club of Paris is focusing the knowledge agenda setting for countries on Societal Innovation (see www.new-club-of-paris.org).

Chairman Ben Bernanke of the U.S. Federal Reserve was addressing some of these same aspects in a key note speech in May 2011 hosted by Georgetown University: http://www.icapitaladvisors.com/2011/05/31/bernanke-on-intangible-capital/. OECD and the World Bank are developing NIC statistics, often based on the model from Corrado–Hultén. Japan has been developing both NIC and Intangible Assets (IA) at METI for some time now. Their research on IC/IA has resulted in a National IA Week with various key stakeholders, such as government agencies, universities, stock exchange, and enterprises. Japan is so far the only country in the world to hold such activities, and they have been doing so for the last 8 years. Australia, Singapore, South Korea, and China are currently undertaking various NIC initiatives. Other countries are also becoming more and more aware of NIC, with policy rhetoric centered on innovation, education, R&D, and trade. Despite this, the map for a more justified NIC navigation has been missing.

This booklet highlights NIC development for a number of countries, based on 48 different indicators, aggregated into four major NIC components of human capital, market capital, process capital, and renewal capital. The model here is a refined and verified statistical model in comparison to the Corrado–Hultén model. We call it the L–E–S model after the contributors Lin–Edvinsson–Stahle. Based on a deeper understanding and the timeline pattern it sets forth, this model will add to a better NIC navigation, not to mention knowledge agenda setting for countries.

Upon looking at a global cluster NIC map, it is evident that the top leading countries seem to be small countries, especially Singapore, the Nordic countries, Hong Kong, and Taiwan. For the U.S., Finland, and Sweden around 50 % or more of its economical growth is related to NIC aspects. Sweden, Finland, Switzerland, the U.S., Israel, and Denmark are strongly influenced in its GDP growth by focusing on Renewal Capital.

It might be that we will see a clearer map of the NIC ecosystem and drivers for wealth emerge in the extension of this ongoing unique research of NIC. This booklet will present a NIC map for various clusters of countries. It can be used for bench marking as well as bench learning for policy prototyping. The starting point is awareness and thinking of NIC, and its drivers for economic results. Based on this more refined navigation, NIC metrics can be presented.

Deeper understanding will emerge from this research, such as the scaling up of limited skilled human capital in one nation by using the globalized broadband technologies for migration and flow of knowledge (such as tele-medicine or mobile banking in Africa). This is also referred to as the IC multiplier. It might also be the way the old British Commonwealth was constructed, but without the IC taxonomy. In modern taxonomy it might be the shaping of NIC alliances for the migration and flow of IC between nations?

Another understanding that might emerge for policy making is the issue of employment versus unemployment. The critical understanding will be deployment of IC drivers. This will require another networked workforce of value networkers on a global scale, such as volunteering software and apps developers. However such volunteers do not show up in traditional statistics, for the mapping on behalf of policymakers.

On another level, there might be a clear gap analyses between nations to support the vision process of a nation. On a deeper level, it is also a leadership responsibility to address the gap of NIC positions versus potential positions. Such a gap is in fact a liability to the citizens, to be addressed in due time.

This will take us to the need for the continuous renewal of social systems. The so-called Arab Spring is explained by some as resulting from three drivers: lack of renewal of social systems, Internet, and soccer as cross class interaction space. The lack of social renewal and innovation is most likely critical early warning signals. For Greece, we can see such a tipping point occurred back in 1999.

On a global scale we might see that the concern for the Euro zone crisis should and can be explained by a deeper and supplementary understanding of NIC, in addition to financial capital. So we need to refine our NIC understanding, NIC mapping, NIC metrics, and NIC organizational constructs into societal innovation for the benefit of wealth creation of subsequent generations.

Leif Edvinsson
The World's First Professor of Intellectual Capital
Chairman and Co-founder of New Club of Paris

Preface II

Our first book *National Intellectual Capital*: *A Comparison of 40 Countries* was published in early 2011, at a time when the 2008 global financial crisis had been declared over yet the European region was still plagued with sovereign debt problems. Before we finalized the book, we were able to retrieve some of our raw data concerning the troubled countries, such as Greece, Iceland, Ireland, Portugal, and Spain. The results of our analysis based on data spanning 1995–2008 revealed some early warning signs of the financial turmoil in those countries. In my preface of that book, I mentioned the warning signs might reveal only the tip of an iceberg. At that time, my co-author, Prof. Edvinsson, and I decided to do a follow up study to trace the development of National Intellectual Capital (NIC) in as many countries as possible, particularly through the lens of the 2008 global financial crisis. This 12 booklet series is the result of that determination.

The 2008 global financial crisis came with unexpected speed and had such a wide-spread effect that surprised many countries far from the epicenter of the initial U.S. sub-prime financial problem, geographically and financially. According to reports, no country was immune from the impact of this financial crisis. Such development clearly signifies how closely connected the world has become and the importance of having a global interdependent view. By reporting what happened during 2005–2010 in 48 major countries throughout the world, this booklet series serves the purpose of uncovering national problems before the crisis, government coping strategies, stimulus plans, potential prospects, and challenges of each individual country, and the interdependence between countries. The 6 years of data allow us to compare NIC and economic development crossing before, during, and after the financial crisis. They are handy booklets for readers to have a quick yet overall view of countries of personal interest. The list of 48 countries in 11 clusters is provided in the appendix of each booklet.

Searching for financial crisis related literature for 48 countries is itself a very daunting task, not to mention summarizing and analyzing it. For financial crisis related literature, we mainly relied on the reports and statistics of certain world organizations, including OECD, World Bank, United Nations, International Monetary Fund (IMF), European Commission Office, the US Congressional Research Service, the U.S. Central Intelligence Agency, and International Labor Office (ILO). Some reliable research centers, such as the National Bureau of

Economic Research in the U.S., World Economic Forum, the Heritage Foundation in the U.S., and government websites from each country were also our sources of information. Due to the requirement of more update and comprehensive information, we were not able to use as much academic literature as we would have liked, because it generally covers a very specific topic with time lag and with research methods not easily comprehended by the general public. Therefore, we had to resort to some online news reports for more current information.

In the middle of 2012, the lasting financial troubles caused the European economy to tilt back into a recession, which also slowed down economic growth across the globe. However, almost 4 years have passed since the outbreak of the global financial crisis in late 2008; it is about time to reflect on what happened and the impact of the financial crisis. By comparing so many countries, we came to a preliminary conclusion that countries with faster recovery from the financial crisis have higher NIC than those with slower recovery. In other words, countries that rebounded fast from the crisis generally have solid NIC fundamentals, including human capital, market capital, process capital, and renewal capital. We also found that the higher the NIC, the higher the GDP per capita (ppp). This booklet series provides a different perspective to look beyond the traditional economic indicators for national development.

In an era when IA have become a key competitive advantage, investing in NIC development is investing in future national development and well-being.

Enjoy!

Carol Yeh-Yun Lin
Professor, Department of Business Administration
National Chengchi University, Taiwan
Taiwan Intellectual Capital Research Center (TICRC)

Executive Summary

Synergy between the new and the old system needs to be achieved during the transformation from central planning to market economy.

One of the key factors of the financial crisis was that conventional financial systems failed to detect potential risks due to non-transparent information disclosure. Our earlier National Intellectual Capital (NIC) research revealed warning signs of impending financial crisis for Greece and Ireland. Such findings indicate that NIC, albeit intangible, can provide valuable insights into risk control and strategy formulation. This booklet looks at the connections between the financial crisis and NIC development for Bulgaria, the Czech Republic, Hungary, Poland, and Romania.

Particularly, this report attempts to answer the following questions: How did NIC facilitate the development of emerging European countries over the last decade? How did they position themselves for long-term sustainability through building intangible NIC? In what way did they weather through the 2008 global financial crisis well enough for future national development? Which country is the model for successful transformation from central planning to market economy? What pattern emerges on NIC as "Capital in Waiting" for these economies?

Data covering 2005–2010 for 48 countries indicate that the *higher the NIC, the higher the GDP per capita (ppp)*, accentuating the value of NIC as a driver in major countries/economies throughout the world. *For the* 6-*year average of NIC rankings among* 48 *countries, Bulgaria ranks* 35, *the Czech Republic*25, *Hungary*29, *Poland* 32, *and Romania*39.

The 2008 financial crisis caused severe impacts all across the globe and is considered to be the worst since the *Great Depression* of the 1930s. The crisis came with unexpected speed and spread into a global economic shock, which resulted in a number of bank failures. During this period, economies worldwide slowed, credits tightened, and international trade declined. In an effort to mitigate the crisis, governments and central banks worldwide responded with unprecedented fiscal stimuli, monetary policy expansions, and institutional bailouts. These measures had its desired impact and the financial crisis was declared over by the end of 2009.

However, the short global recovery in 2010 was overshadowed by the lingering sovereign debt problems in Europe, thus a global economic slowdown recurred in the second half of 2011. Despite the efforts of Euro leaders to prevent large economies like Italy and Spain from needing a bailout, Spain still asked for external financial assistance in June 2012. As of late 2012, economic recovery in most developed countries was still hampered by the weak global development.

The five emerging European economies reported in this volume have close connection with advanced European countries, especially with respect to the banking industry. As a result, these emerging countries were hard hit by the 2008 global financial crisis. Over the 6 years between 2005 and 2010, Hungary had a relatively sharp *GDP growth* decline in 2007, followed by the Czech Republic in 2008. In 2009, all had negative GDP growth, except Poland. With each government's coping stimulus package and the financial assistance from EU and International Monetary Fund (IMF), all five countries except Romania experienced a GDP growth rebound in 2010.

In 2005, the levels of general *government debt* in these emerging European countries were generally within the EU standard of less than 60 % GDP, with Hungary (61.77 %) over a little. However in 2010, Hungary's government debt level of 80.2 % was far above the other four countries of below 55 %. Over the 6 years, Bulgaria is the only country that had reduced government debt, comparing its 2010 and 2005 levels. On the contrary, Romania shows a drastic debt increase when comparing its level in 2005 (13.38 %) and that in 2010 (30.76 %).

Aside from GDP growth and government debt, *unemployment* is another important indicator to check the degree of financial crisis impact. The unemployment rate of these five countries was relatively stable during the 6-year period and was not as devastating as that in the Southern European countries. In this country cluster, rather than from 2008, the unemployment increase started from 2009 showing the spillover effects of the financial troubles in advanced European countries. After the financial crisis, Hungary was the only country with the rate increase—from 7.2 % in 2005 to 11.2 % in 2010. In contrast, Poland reduced unemployment from 17.7 % in 2005 to 9.6 % in 2010. The other three countries generally maintained their 2005 unemployment rate in 2010. For *consumer price inflation* (CPI), the hiked inflation in 2008 in each country was under control in 2009 and 2010. During the 6 years, Bulgaria had the highest CPI of 12.3 % in 2008, yet it was reduced to below 3 % in 2009 and 2010. Romania had the highest CPI in both 2005 and 2010 among the five countries.

In these five emerging European countries, the Czech Republic and Hungary are the two countries that were the *forerunners of transforming* from a central planned economy to a market economy. These two countries also had higher NIC compared to the other three countries. In particular, market capital of the Czech Republic ranks 18th among 48 countries. For the co-development of each individual capital and GDP ppp, the Czech Republic was consistently the best performer, followed by Hungary, Poland, and then Bulgaria and Romania with intertwined development. Specifically, Bulgaria was better in market capital, process capital, and financial capital than Romania. On the other hand, Romania was better in human capital and renewal capital than Bulgaria. That is, Romania was stronger in long-term NIC than Bulgaria and has a great potential to surpass Bulgaria in the future.

For the *dynamic NIC ranking* changes in three time periods (2005–2006, 2007–2008, 2009–2010), the ranking gains represent increasing international competitiveness (among the 48 countries) after the financial crisis. Bulgaria lost its human capital and renewal capital competitiveness, so did the Czech Republic in market capital after the financial crisis. Hungary had the most noticeable ranking losses in market capital and NIC. On the contrary, *Poland had the most noticeable ranking gains in market capital and NIC*. Romania had ranking gains in process capital and NIC.

The NIC 3D *trajectory analysis* was conducted to detect the enhancing and impeding factors of each country in reaching a targeted GDP ppp, benchmarking Germany due to its leading economic development in Europe. To reach German GDP level, the Czech Republic has the shortest distance (47.63 %) to cover, followed by Romania (55.82 %), Hungary (56.41 %), Poland (60.51 %), and Bulgaria (77.85 %) (see Table 3.4). Interestingly, even though Hungary ranks number two in NIC development among the five countries, its route to reach Germany's GDP level requires a longer distance than Romania—the GDP per capita (ppp) laggard in this country cluster. In addition, Bulgaria has the longest distance to cover despite its better position in market capital, process capital, and financial capital than Romania. This set of statistics indicates the potential of Romania in its national development.

As of late 2012, the world economic recovery has been hampered by the pending debt problems in the Euro zone, the modest growth in the U.S., and the slowdown growth in Asia. The economies of these five emerging European countries were again affected and exhibited slower growth. Each economy's resilience to crisis will again be tested if the world plunges back into recession.

This economic crisis provides an ideal opportunity for nations to examine/renew/innovate the soundness of their economic system and the effectiveness of *national governance related to NIC*. The following implications are drawn from our research findings. Readers can refer to Chap. 5 for the rationale behind these implications.

1. NIC development goes together with the economic development and should be regarded as an enhancer of economic growth.
2. Achieving financial independence should have a time table, as EU and IMF financial aid will stop someday.
3. Synergy between the new and the old system is critical for a successful transformation from central planning to market economy.
4. More effective national and NIC governance systems need to be established, such as over regulation and corruption.
5. Visionary and responsible public servants need to be cultivated and experts need to be involved with national development.

6. Strategies between focus and diversification need to be weighed for effective national and NIC development.
7. Investment in research and development is the key source of future competitiveness for these emerging European countries.
8. To speed up future Euro currency adoption, continuous structural reform is essential.

In the coming decade, economic development in emerging regions will still catch worldwide attention, including the countries reported in this volume. This report uncovers that in this country cluster the forerunners of the market economy—the Czech Republic and Hungary—had higher GDP ppp as well as better NIC. That is, the strength of their economy was accompanied by better NIC. In addition, NIC is "Capital in Waiting" for these economies and a nation's responsibility is to have policies taking it from "Capital in Waiting" to "Capital in Action," such as Poland and the Czech Republic. In an era when the intangible asset has become a key competitive advantage, investing in NIC development is in essence investing in future economic development and well-being. NIC evolution should be nourished both from local culture viewpoint as well as global interconnectivity by social media.

Based on the emerging new insights of values, societal history as well as citizen relationships, a key focus for the future will be on the fusion of NIC and social service innovation as well as societal innovation, for the enabling of a new societal fabric.

Contents

List of Figures

List of Tables

Appendices

Abstract

In the first decade of the new millennium, the biggest event that caught worldwide attention was the 2008 global financial crisis, which was brought about primarily by ineffective governance, failed surveillance systems, and implementation flaws. These problems are mainly intangible in nature. Therefore, examining the financial crisis from the viewpoint of intangible asset provides a different perspective from traditional economic approaches.

National intellectual capital (NIC), mainly consisting of human capital, market capital, process capital, renewal capital, and financial capital, is a valuable intangible asset and a key source of national competitive advantage in today's knowledge economy. This booklet looks into the connections between the 2008 global financial crisis and NIC development with a special focus on Bulgaria, the Czech Republic, Hungary, Poland, and Romania.

In addition to the summaries of financial crisis impact, the aftermath, future prospects, and challenges of each individual country, NIC analysis based on data covering 2005–2010 for 48 countries reveal that the higher the NIC, the higher the GDP per capita (ppp). Graphical presentations of various types allow for intra-country and inter-country comparisons to position the reported five countries on a world map of NIC–GDP co-development.

By looking into tangible economic development along with intangible NIC development, this booklet provides valuable implications for policymakers.

Keywords Competitiveness · Economic policy · Financial capital · Human capital · Innovation · Intangible assets · Intellectual capital · Knowledge management · Research and development (R&D) · Science and technology policy

Chapter 1
Introduction

The 2008 global financial crisis is considered by many economists to be the worst one since the Great Depression of the 1930s. The crisis rapidly developed and spread into a global economic shock, which resulted in a number of European bank failures (Altman 2009; Fackler 2008). World political leaders, national ministers of finance, and central bank directors coordinated their efforts to reduce fear, but the crisis continued and eventually led to a global currency crisis.

Unexpectedly, what started off as sub-prime mortgage problems in the financial sector in the U.S. snowballed into the deepest and most widespread financial and economic crisis in the last several decades. With almost synchronized worldwide recession, global Gross Domestic Product (GDP) contracted for the first time since World War II, according to the International Monetary Fund (IMF). Governments and central banks around the world have responded to the crisis through both conventional and unconventional fiscal and monetary measures in order to maintain financial order as well as help industries, private companies, and citizens wade through the difficulties.

In 2009, the World Bank estimated that the 2008 global financial crisis would create an additional 53 million people in poverty who live on less than US$2 per day, due mainly to the decline of global economic growth. The magnitude of this crisis is so large that it has disrupted the global financial system and as a result there is no single economy in the world that is completely isolated from the effect of the crisis.

In the wake of the crisis, causes of the disaster have become known although its impact varies from country to country after combining with local factors. Briefly speaking, the initial collapse of sub-prime bonds in the U.S. resulted in a shortage in the global money market. As a result, huge amounts of foreign investments were withdrawn from the invested countries all over the world to increase their home companies' liquidity. Thus, the credit squeeze affected domestic market operations. Due to very negative cash flows, many companies slashed their production levels and cancelled or postponed investment projects (Mendonça 2010). With a tight money market, export demands dropped and unemployment increased. Adding to the problem was that some European Union countries were overlending and overspending even before 2008. Consequently, banks in many countries did

C. Y.-Y. Lin et al., *National Intellectual Capital and the Financial Crisis in Bulgaria, Czech Republic, Hungary, Romania, and Poland*, SpringerBriefs in Economics,
DOI: 10.1007/978-1-4614-8018-1_1, © The Author(s) 2014

not have enough money to support the repayment of foreign debts and corporate loans. Thus, confidence fell, which directly hit the consumer market, and a global financial crisis set in.

During the early stages of the financial crisis, management scholars criticized the traditional accounting system's inability to reveal the intangibles that explain hidden risks as well as values for proper decision making (Reavis 2009). In line with the importance of the intangibles, intellectual capital (Edvinsson and Malone 1997) advocating the value of human capital, social capital, and the like has gained increasing attention in today's keener global competition.

It is our deep belief that national intellectual capital, albeit intangible, can provide valuable insights to policy makers regarding future risk control and strategy formulation. Our previous book, *National Intellectual Capital: A Comparison of 40 Countries* (Lin and Edvinsson 2011; www.nic40.org), was born out of this belief and traces the national intellectual capital development of 40 countries over a 14-year period from 1995 to 2008. The data analysis presented in our previous work revealed certain warning signs of impending financial crisis for countries such as Greece, Iceland, and Ireland (Lin and Edvinsson 2011; 327–333). As a follow up study, this booklet series is an attempt to further understand the connections between the 2008 global financial crisis and national intellectual capital (NIC) development.

The booklet series, in its entirety, will examine the NIC statuses of 48 countries from the period of 2005–2010 to glean new understanding about whether there is a NIC development pattern that distinguishes fast recovery countries from slow recovery ones. This is presented through a series of 11 country clusters, with each booklet focusing on one particular cluster. The clusters are determined based on several factors: geographical proximity, size, and phase of economic development. Focusing on one cluster at a time, we probe the issues of concern within a single country and extend to compare multiple countries to see whether the situation before and after the crisis can be explained by the intangible NIC. Our data comes from the well-recognized International Institute for Management Development (IMD) in Switzerland. The IMD has been publishing yearly rankings of World Competitiveness for around two decades. Hopefully, the analysis in this booklet series can provide a different perspective of the financial crisis for future policy implications.

This volume—Volume Six will focus on five emerging European countries of Bulgaria, the Czech Republic, Hungary, Poland, and Romania as they are countries behind the iron curtain after World War II and are transforming from central planning to market economies. In addition, they are geographically close to each other, thus have economic, market, and inherent similarities that make it easy to compare and examine them as a cluster.

This booklet first provides an economic background to these five countries as a whole before going into each individual country's development. Through this process, the authors hope to paint a general picture of the economic condition and provide a basis for our dataset and analysis in future sections. Next, Chap. 2 briefly introduces the impact of 2008 financial crisis on each individual country.

Chapter 3 discusses the NIC development of these five countries. Chapter 4 describes issues beyond the financial crisis and Chap. 5 concludes with future perspectives and policy implications.

Economic Background

This volume particularly focuses on past Communist European countries, which were behind the iron curtain dominated by the old Soviet Union until their transformation to market economies. They are Bulgaria, the Czech Republic, Hungary, Poland, and Romania. The following brief introduction of each country is mainly based on the background information provided by the U.S. Central Intelligence Agency (CIA 2012).

Bulgaria fell within the old Soviet influence after World War II (WWII). Its communist domination ended in 1990, with the first multiparty election since WWII and began the contentious process of moving toward political democracy and a market economy. The country joined NATO in 2004 and the EU in 2007. Czechoslovakia was also under the Soviet influence after the WWII. With the collapse of Soviet-backed authority in 1989, the country regained its democracy. However, the "velvet divorce" split the country into two national components, the Czech Republic and Slovakia. The Czech Republic joined NATO in 1999 and the European Union in 2004. Hungary was also under Communist rule following WWII. In 1968, Hungary began liberalizing its economy and held its first multi-party elections in 1990 for a free market economy. It joined NATO in 1999 and the EU 5 years later. Poland became a Soviet satellite state following the WWII. Labor turmoil in 1980 led to the formation of the independent trade union "Solidarity" that later became a political force. After free elections in 1989 and 1990, Solidarity took control of the parliament and the presidency, thus ended the Communist era. A fast pace reform during the early 1990s enabled the country to transform its economy into one of the most robust in Central Europe. Poland joined NATO in 1999 and the EU in 2004. Romania participated in the 1941 German invasion of the USSR and was overrun by the Soviets after the WWII. Former Communists dominated the government until 1996. Romania joined NATO in 2004 and the EU in 2007.

The dissolution of Soviet power brought a sudden collapse of Eastern Europe's Communist governments, which inspired dreams and expectations. However, as one Czech economist said in 1990, "It will take 10–15 years for us just to approach, not to equal, living standards in Austria and other Western countries," the voyage from the communist central planning to free markets is lengthy and painful (Greenhouse 1990). During the past two decades of economic, social, and political transformation, there were crises as well as prosperities in this region. Each country has its unique form of development. Through the lens of viewing how they cope with the 2008 global financial crisis, this booklet partially unveils the national development of these five countries in the past and their potential future.

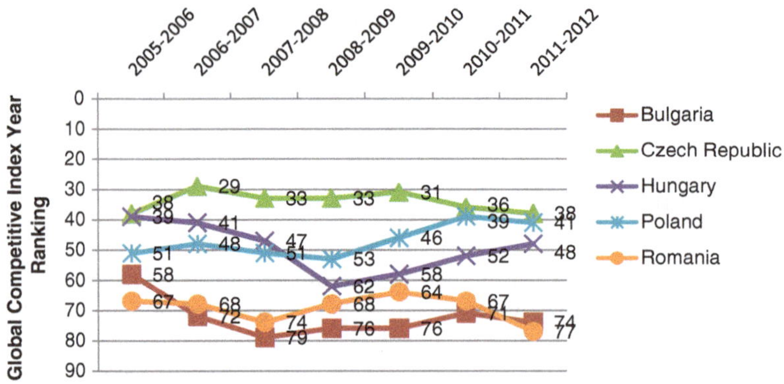

Fig. 1.1 GCI ranking of the five east European countries

To paint a general picture of these five countries' global competitiveness in the most recent years and before the financial crisis, we introduce hereunder the Global Competitiveness Index (GCI) published by the World Economic Forum for the reader's reference. This index is relatively robust as it takes into account the 12 distinct pillars[1] containing basic requirements, efficiency enhancers, and innovation factors that contribute to a nation's overall economic strength. Based upon commonly accepted economic theory, the development of a total 142 countries was split into three stages in which different factors play the dominant role in determining the outcome of a country's economy. Stage 1, Stage 2, and Stage 3 are respectively characterized by being factor, efficiency, and innovation driven (Schwab 2011). Bulgaria and Romania were categorized as Stage 2 countries, Hungary and Poland were transitioned from Stage 2 to Stage 3 countries, and Czech Republic was a Stage 3 country.

Plotting each country's annual ranking against a time series of seven periods, Fig. 1.1 displays a rough pictorial overview of the five economies' global competitiveness before and after the financial crisis. As an indicator of economic strength in 2011–2012, Bulgaria ranks #74, the Czech Republic #38, Hungary #48, Poland #41, and Romania #77, respectively.

From Fig. 1.1, it can be seen that over the past 7 years, only Poland advanced its global competitiveness ranking from 51 to 41 and the Czech Republic remained the same ranking at 38. The other three countries had global competitiveness decline, with Bulgaria having the greatest drop from ranking 58 to 74. These results largely reflect the pace of recovery after the 2008 global financial crisis in these five countries.

[1] The 12 pillars include: institutions, infrastructure, macroeconomic environment, health and primary education, higher education and training, goods market efficiency, labor market efficiency, financial market development, technological readiness, market size, business sophistication, and innovation.

In September 2011, OECD reported that major economies were tilting back into recession as the sovereign debt problems continued to ail the Euro zone (Bryant 2011). IMF (2012a) also announced that global growth prospects were dimmed and risks sharply escalated as the Euro area crisis entered a perilous new phase in January 2012. Particularly, growth in emerging and developing economies slowed more than forecasted, reflecting the deterioration in the external environment and the slowdown of domestic markets in major emerging economies. The adverse spillover effects are expected to be largest for central and eastern Europe, given the region's strong trade and financial linkages with the Euro area economies (IMF 2012a).

The 2012 Spring World Economic Outlook of the IMF has reduced the economic growth projection for Bulgaria by almost half to 0.8 % in 2012, down from its fall 2011 projection of 1.3 % (Novinite 2012). For the Czech Republic, OECD projected its real GDP fall in 2012 owing to a decline in domestic consumption spurred by fiscal consolidation; however, growth will return in 2013 due to stronger exports and investment (OECD 2012a). Hungary has a weak currency, rising oil prices and hikes in indirect taxes; thus its economy is also expected to decline in 2012; however growth should return in 2013 (OECD 2012e). Poland is the champion in Emerging Europe with a growth of 2.6 % in 2012 and 3.2 % in 2013, whereas Romania was projected to have a growth of 1.5 % in 2012 and of 3 % in 2013 (Novinite 2012).

The next chapter will give a brief background and qualitative analysis of the financial crisis as it relates to these five countries.

Chapter 2
Impact of the 2008 Financial Crisis

In order to present the impact of the 2008 financial crisis, this chapter first describes the common problems in these five countries. Next, it graphically compares the GDP growth, total general government debt, unemployment rate, and consumer price inflation of the five economies during the time period from 2005 to 2010. Then, it elaborates on its impact on each country individually in the sequence of Bulgaria, the Czech Republic, Hungary, Poland, and Romania.

At the onset of the financial crisis, many countries viewed it as a purely American sub-prime mortgage problem. Yet, the crisis rapidly developed and spread into a global economic shock. This resulted in the U.S. government bailing out several large financial institutions, such as AIG, Fannie Mae, Freddie Mac. In addition, coupled with the trouble in America, a number of European banks also failed and stock markets declined across the board (Altman 2009; Fackler 2008). The Emerging European countries, including the five reported in this volume were directly impacted with the largest adverse effect owing to their heavy export dependence on the EU countries. With the trade drastically dropped, credit tightened, and direct foreign investments rapidly withdrawn, these five countries were hit hard by the 2008 global financial crisis.

Following the outbreak of the financial crisis, in late 2008, the European Union proposed an European stimulus plan amounting to around US$256 billion or 1.5 % of the European Union's GDP—around 1.2 % of GDP from national budgets and the rest 0.3 % of GDP from EU and European Investment Bank budgets (Europa 2008). For the entire world, the estimated US$2 trillion total in stimulus packages amounted to approximately 3 % of world Gross Domestic Product. This exceeded the call by the IMF for fiscal stimulus by 2 % of global GDP (Nanto 2009).

Eastern Europe has experienced increased financial integration with the West with a large amount of foreign direct investment inflows even prior to the eastern countries' accession to the EU. As of the end of 2001, 41 major EU15 banking groups had 15 branches and 76 subsidiaries in Eastern Europe (Nanto 2009; World Bank 2011). For European and U.K. banks, cross-border lending to emerging markets, primarily Central and Eastern Europe accounts for between 21 and 24 % of total lending (Nanto 2009). The quickness with which the 2008 global financial

C. Y.-Y. Lin et al., *National Intellectual Capital and the Financial Crisis in Bulgaria, Czech Republic, Hungary, Romania, and Poland*, SpringerBriefs in Economics,
DOI: 10.1007/978-1-4614-8018-1_2, © The Author(s) 2014

crisis has impacted emerging market economies has taken many analysts by surprise, with Central and Eastern Europe appear to be the most vulnerable due to its high financial integration with the European countries (Nanto 2009; World Bank 2011). Yet, banks in some countries such as the Czech Republic did better than others during the global economic crisis (World Bank 2011). Romania and Bulgaria—two most recent entrants into the European Union, in 2007—were all running current account deficits in double digits and Poland had the consistently lowest deficits around −1 to −5 % of GDP (Kattel 2010).

The financial freeze thus immediately exposed critical flaw in several countries' economic policy—strong and unhedged reliance on short-term financing of long-term projects. Exchange rates of the Czech Republic, Hungary, and Poland fluctuated wildly in the second half of 2008 (Schneider 2009). Hungary and Romania encountered serious financing problems and had to turn to the IMF for support (Terazi and Senel 2011). On October 28, 2008 the IMF announced a US$15.7 billion package for Hungary and on May 4, 2009 it approved a 24-month Stand-By Arrangement in the amount of US$17.1 billion (€12.95 billion) for Romania (IMF 2009; Nanto 2009). For countries with strong fundamentals, policies, and track records of policy implementation, the IMF also created a Flexible Credit Line. Under this facility, the IMF board has approved US$20.5 billion for Poland (Nanto 2009).

The impact of the 2008 global financial crisis on each country can be easily observed from the following four graphs, namely the percentage of real GDP growth per capita, total general government debt percentage of GDP, unemployment rate of labor force, and consumer price inflation.

Comparisons of the Five Countries

This section presents four graphs in order to examine the five emerging European countries as a whole from 2005 to 2010. Figure 2.1 shows that all the countries had a drastic decline in *real GDP growth* in 2009, except Poland. The GDP growth of Bulgaria and Romania has the similar pattern, having relatively good and stable growth from 2005 to 2008, then rapidly dropped in 2009 and rebounded in 2010. The Czech Republic had an early decline in 2008 with a continuous drop in 2009. Hungary started off with the lowest GDP growth in 2005 and its economy stalled as early as 2007 with less than 1 % growth, then drastically dropped in 2009 with relatively good rebound in 2010. Poland is the champion in this country cluster, still having positive growth in 2009.

In terms of the total *general government debt* as a percentage of the GDP, Fig. 2.2 indicates that Bulgaria started off with the second lowest amount of government debt, next to Romania in 2005. Its debt level reached the lowest in 2008 and afterwards carried the lowest debt in this country cluster. The Czech Republic and Poland had the similar pattern with relatively stable government debt from 2005 to 2008 and then increased a little in 2009 and 2010. However, Poland has about a 20 % point higher debt level than that of the Czech Republic. Hungary

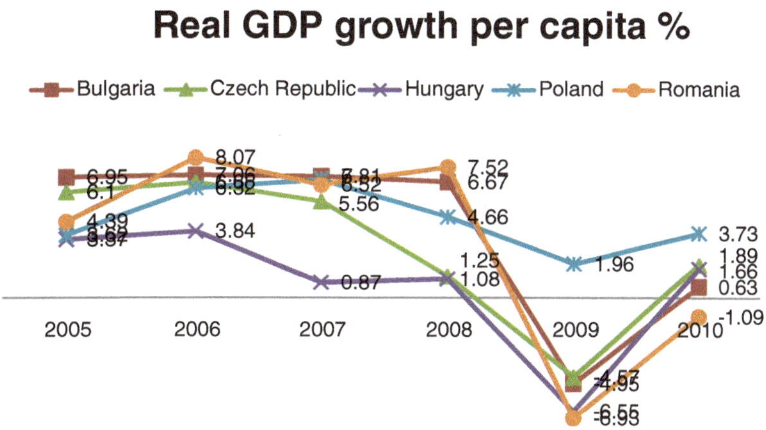

Fig. 2.1 Real GDP growth per capita of the five eastern European countries from 2005 to 2010

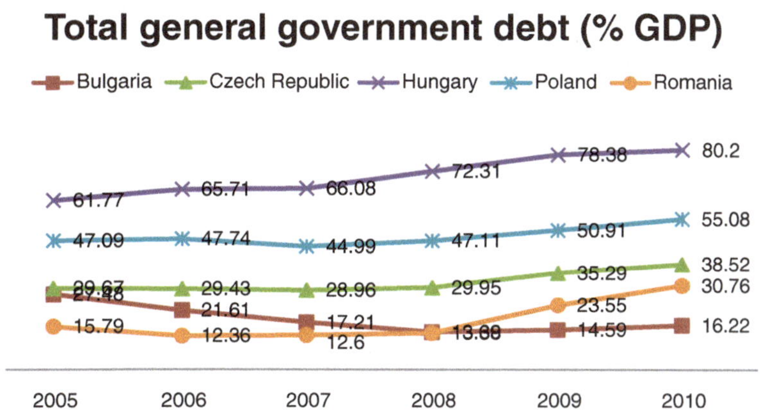

Fig. 2.2 Total general government debt (% GDP) of the five eastern European countries from 2005 to 2010

had the highest government debt over the 6 years with continuous rising debt level, reaching more than 80 % of GDP in 2010. Romania has the lowest government debt in 2005, however its debt level increased with a relatively large scale in 2009 and 2010, reaching over 30 % of GDP reflecting its increasing financial needs after the financial crisis.

Reinhart and Rogoff (2009) reported findings from their research on financial crises over the last 800 years that the aftermath of a financial crisis brings slow and halted growth, sustained high unemployment, and surging public debt—with the overhang of public and private debt being the most important impediment to a normal recovery from the recession.

Figure 2.3 shows that the *unemployment* rate of the five countries did not fluctuate too much over the 6 years, except Poland started off with a very high rate of 17.7 % in 2005. However, it dropped rapidly in 4 years and reduced to 7.1 % in 2008, not too far apart from that of its neighboring countries. Unexpectedly, in 2008 all the countries, except Hungary, had their lowest unemployment rate in 6 years. However, their rates rose in 2009 and 2010, reflecting the influence of the sovereign debt problems in the Euro zone rather than the ripple effect of the U.S. sub-prime financial problem in 2008.

Figure 2.4 shows relatively large-scale ups and downs of *consumer price inflation* (CPI) in these five countries over 6 years. 2008 was an "up" year for these countries, except Hungary, mainly due to a rising economy for several consecutive years. Then inflation apparently cooled down with the recession in 2009, except in Poland. Bulgaria and the Czech Republic were able to reduce CPI in 2010 to lower than its 2005 level. In 2010, Hungary had a higher CPI and Poland regained a CPI comparable to 2005. Romania started off with the highest inflation and remained the same in 2010.

In general, the four figures shown above indicate that real GDP growth and CPI were apparently impacted by the financial and ensuing sovereign debt crisis. General government debt and unemployment rate were relatively unaffected. Aside from the impact of the crisis, in this country cluster Bulgaria had good real GDP growth, low general government debt, a fair unemployment rate, and a stabilized CPI (after the financial crisis). The Czech Republic had real GDP growth decrease starting in 2008, low general government debt, a low unemployment rate, and a stabilized CPI (after the financial crisis). Hungary was a poor performer in this country cluster with low real GDP growth, the highest general government debt, a continuously rising unemployment rate, yet a stabilized CPI

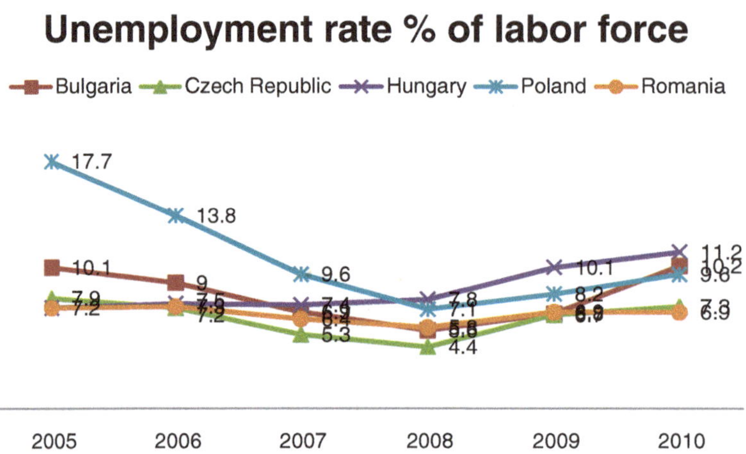

Fig. 2.3 Unemployment rate % of labor force of the five eastern European countries from 2005 to 2010

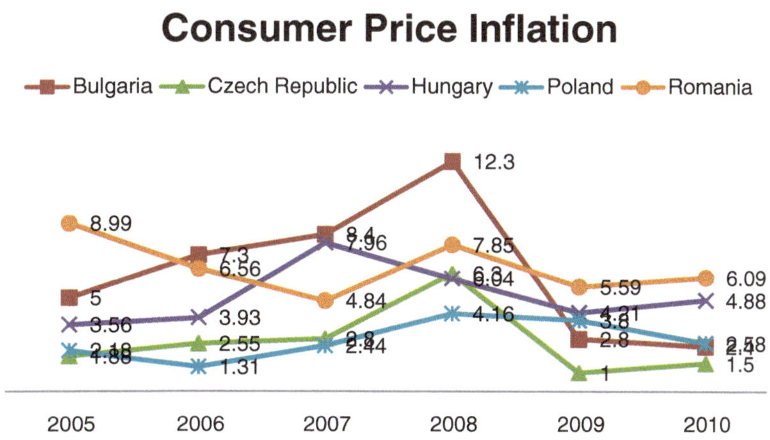

Fig. 2.4 Consumer price inflation of the five eastern European countries from 2005 to 2010

(after the financial crisis). Poland is the best performer in this country cluster, except its high unemployment rate from 2005 to 2007and middle level of general government debt of around 50 % GDP. Romania had good real GDP growth before the financial crisis, low general government debt, a low unemployment rate, and a stabilized yet high CPI (after the financial crisis).

In what follows, we briefly describe the impact of the 2008 global financial crisis on these five emerging European countries. The depth of the report depends on the English literature available for each economy. For readers to gain a general picture about the efforts that each economy has put into mitigating the negative impact of the financial crisis, we have summarized the details of stimulus packages implemented by the five countries in Appendix 1. Please note that the reported package is based on publicly available data and is not an exhaustive list. In addition, the reported amount of stimulus package was based on the exchange rate at the time of each stimulus, and thus varies. Readers can also refer to Appendix 2 for the important meetings conducted by key global leaders during this financial crisis.

Bulgaria

Bulgaria, in line with the vast inflow of capital since the signing of an EU accession agreement in 2004, has implemented substantial economic reforms and made considerable progress in income growth and poverty reduction. Its competitive flat tax rates, open trade, and a relatively efficient regulatory framework have encouraged the development of a growing entrepreneurial sector. Driven by significant amounts of foreign direct investment (FDI) and consumption, the country experienced more than 6 % annual growth from 2004 to 2008 (CIA 2012; Heritage 2012). In 2008, Bulgaria registered the lowest unemployment rate within the past 10 years (Stoilov 2009).

However, the robust economic activity was also accompanied by an overheated economy, private debt due to strong consumption, and substantial inflationary pressures (European Union 2010; QFinance 2012a; Social Watch 2010). The FDI-led investment boom and high wage increases, far exceeding productivity gains, has aggravated the imbalances (European Union 2010).

Before the outburst of the 2008 global financial crisis, Bulgaria has several strong starting conditions including a low level of government debt, budgetary surpluses, and a sound financial system which was not exposed to toxic assets (CSD, n.d.). Nevertheless, Bulgaria remains excessively vulnerable to external shocks, mainly due to the high level of foreign trade, banks, and FDI integration with the EU (Angelov 2009). For instance, combined assets of commercial banks exceed 100 % of GDP, among which foreign banks account for more than 80 % of total assets and the three largest banks account for more than 30 % of assets (Heritage 2012). Other vulnerabilities include the institutional uncertainty, higher levels of the hidden economy, corruption and crime, overpriced real estate assets, over 90 % GDP of private external debt, and loss of competitiveness (CSD, n.d.).

In Bulgaria, consolidation began in 2004 with high privatization of state-owned banks. The introduction of a currency board, stronger supervision, and tighter prudential rules have also helped to transform Bulgaria's banking sector (Heritage 2012). Bulgaria enjoyed 12 years of consecutive growth until 2009 (QFinance 2012a). As the global economic crisis unfolded, Bulgaria's economic activity was hit hard, resulting in a 5 % contraction of real GDP in 2009 (CIA 2012; European Union 2010; Social Watch 2010).

Bulgaria felt the impact of the financial and economic crisis at the end of 2008 (Minassian 2011). The FDI inflows in the first 10 months of 2008 decreased by 9.2 % compared to the same period a year before and the country lost about 12,000 jobs in the last 4 months in 2008 (Dikov 2009). Although banks in Bulgaria did not fail nor did they need a bailout due to their high level of capital and liquidity, the country's real economy was still badly hit (Angelov 2009). Growth rate in manufacturing slowed down from double-digit in 2007 to 7.1 % in the first half of 2008, and in the third quarter of 2008 manufacturing output declined (Ersado 2009). For 30 months (since January 2009 till June 2011) residents have transferred out of Bulgaria a total of US$3.4 billion (€2.5 billion), about half of these financial resources represent portfolio investments abroad by local institutional investors, and the other half deposits (Minassian 2011). In July 2009, authorities announced emergency measures, including a 15 % cut in the budget of most government departments, freezes on public wages in 2010, and scaled back pension and health care spending (Heritage 2012; QFinance 2012a).

Bulgaria did not adopt a short-term fiscal stimulus package in response to the economic slowdown. Taking into account, the wide macroeconomic imbalances prior to the downturn, the country's policy effort was geared toward fiscal consolidation measures, notably by restricting expenditures and improving tax compliance (European Union 2010). In the second half of 2009, the authorities implemented a fiscal consolidation package amounting to 2.3 % of GDP (European Union 2010). The main points of the package were aimed at maintaining tight fiscal policy and preserving the country's currency board arrangement tying the lev (Bulgaria's currency) to the Euro at a fixed rate. The Bulgarian government planned to achieve a balanced budget in both 2009 and 2010 via stricter control of revenue collecting agencies and cuts in government administration and spending (Mihaylova 2009). Several measures were targeted at improving the business climate, including a 2.0 % cut in social security contributions from 2010 and a reduction of the minimum capital to set up a new company. Another target in the government's plan was to manage EU money more effectively to improve infrastructure and to help farmers (Mihaylova 2009). Around US$3.66 billion (5.6 billion levs) went into infrastructure projects, public building repairs, education, and healthcare-related projects (Reuters 2009).

Bulgaria has weathered the impact of the global economic downturn relatively well, with the economy supported by generally prudent fiscal policy and sound public debt management (Heritage 2012). Strong banking supervision and prudential regulations lessened the impact of global financial turmoil (Heritage 2012). The capital adequacy ratio of the banking system is high (17 % at the end of 2009) and well above the regulatory minimum of 12 % and the EU minimum of 8 %; the coverage ratio of nonperforming loans by provisions exceeded 80 %; and banks continued to report profits in 2009 (QFinance 2012a).

In September 2009, the Bulgarian central bank announced that the current account had moved into surplus for the first time in 5 years, reflecting a fall in consumer spending. The country registered a current account surplus for July 2009 of €102 million, compared to a €439 million current account deficit in July 2008 (QFinance 2012a). In the first 7 months of 2009, the current account gap fell to 7.2 % of the projected GDP, from more than 14 % in the same period of 2008. The recession has also led to a dramatic reduction in inflation, which fell from almost 15 % in June 2008 to 1.3 % in August 2009 (QFinance 2012a).

The Czech Republic

The Czech Republic is a stable and prosperous market economy, which harmonized its laws and regulations with those of the EU prior to its EU accession in 2004 (CIA 2012). The country has been among the world's most industrialized states (Heritage 2012). The small, open, export-driven Czech economy is very sensitive to changes in the economic performance of its main export markets, especially Germany. When Western Europe and Germany fell into recession in late 2008, demand for Czech goods plunged, leading to double digit drops in industrial production and exports (CIA 2012; IMF 2008). The growing integration of the Czech trade and financial sector with the rest of Europe plus the very high level of foreign ownership of the banking sector caused the negative spillover on its economy (IMF 2008). Its exports contracted by 11 % in October, by 18 %, 14 %, and even by 24 % in November, December 2008, and January 2009, respectively (Schneider 2009). GDP growth collapsed from 5 % in early 2008 to 0.7 % in the last quarter of 2008, and real GDP fell more than 4 % in 2009, with most of the decline occurring during the first quarter (CIA 2012; OECD 2010a; Schneider 2009).

The Czech Republic entered into the recession in a relatively good position. The government's current account deficit was very low between 1 and 2 % of GDP at safe level (Schneider 2009). The trade balance was in surplus and the modest current account deficit is expected to be comfortably financed by direct investment inflows (IMF 2008). Export competitiveness was adequate, especially as the koruna (Czech currency) depreciation through the aggressive action of the Czech National Bank offset the adverse impact from the earlier appreciation on profit margins (IMF 2008).

However, Czech's current account worsened throughout 2008 and the deficit for the whole year reached 3.2 % of the GDP, the worst since 2000. In addition, investment rates fell into the negative in the second half of 2008 (Schneider 2009). On the production side, most major sectors contracted. Manufacturing alone accounted for around half the total drop in gross value added, and service sectors linked to the cycle in manufacturing, like trade and transport, were also hit hard (OECD 2010a). Industry, which represents one-third of the Czech economy, began to shed employees in early 2009. In March 2009, the unemployment rate went to almost 8 %, 2 % points above its 2008 levels (Schneider 2009). The country recorded a rapid decline of 63 % in the number of newly created jobs (5,626 jobs in comparison with 15,102 in 2007) (Ernst and Young 2009). Although Czech's consumption held steady in 2008, private consumption growth turned negative in the third quarter of 2009.

In an effort to address the unfolding crisis, the Czech government in late 2008 and early 2009 adopted a range of fiscal stimulus measures, amounting to about 2.2 % of the 2008 GDP, spread across 2009–2010 (OECD 2010a). The package contained US$3.3 billion (72 billion koruna) announced in February 2009 and additional US$1.99 billion (40 billion koruna) announced in April 2009 (Reuters 2009). The stimulus primarily targeted the supply side and aimed at reducing non-wage labor costs to curb employment losses, mitigating the investment contraction, and supporting exports by providing guarantees. At the onset of the financial crisis, the government swiftly implemented a car scrapping scheme to save the auto industry, as it is the largest single industry and together with its suppliers, accounts for as much as 20 % of Czech manufacturing (CIA 2012). However, the stimulus measures were estimated to push the fiscal deficit "significantly" above 3 % of GDP (Reuters 2009). When the budget balance deteriorated faster than had been anticipated, the Czech government projected deficits of 6.6 % for 2009 in the third quarter of 2009 (OECD 2010a).

During the financial crisis, the Czech banking sector was only modestly affected (Heritage 2012). Czech banks did not require bailouts and managed to remain profitable during the financial crisis; in 2009, return on equity amounted to 26.4 % and the return of assets stood at 1.5 % (World Bank 2011). The resilience of the banking system reflected a number of factors, including prudent macroeconomic management, conservative strategies, high levels of liquidity, low inflation, low interest rate (little incentive to borrow in foreign currency), healthy profits from "normal" banking business (minimum dependence on funds from foreign markets), and the lessons drawn from its past banking crises (OECD 2010a; Valert 2008; World Bank 2011). In addition, the subsidiaries of foreign banks did not invest in "toxic" assets, even if their foreign parents did so (OECD 2010a). Furthermore, Czech's early savings have helped to create a cushion for a cyclical margin to stay within the Stability and Growth Pact threshold deficit of 3 % of the GDP (IMF 2008).

In the second quarter of 2009, the Czech real GDP turned around, driven by a slight pickup in exports (CIA 2012; OECD 2010a). The export recovery seems to have owed much to the adoption of car scrapping schemes and other measures to support the automobile sector in major export markets, in addition to the world trade recovery (OECD 2010a). It is interesting to note that this stability was accompanied by a high level of banking sector integration with the rest of Europe; as of January 2010, 96 % of bank assets were foreign owned (World Bank 2011). In addition, its strong fundamentals, such as past robust productivity growth, improved fiscal performance, and a comfortable external position supported by inflows of foreign direct investment have helped the country weather the financial turmoil relatively well (Heritage 2012; IMF 2008).

Hungary

Hungary is the former showcase of an East-European transition from a centrally planned to a market economy (Draper et al. 2009), with a per capita income nearly two-thirds that of the EU-25 average. The share of foreign trade in its GDP reached more than 150 % and almost three-quarters of manufactured goods were exported (Inotai 2010). The private sector accounts for more than 80 % of GDP and cumulative foreign direct investment worth more than US$70 billion (CIA 2012). In the most recent year, total government expenditures, including consumption and transfer payments, were 49.2 % of its GDP (Heritage 2012).

Hungary was not directly exposed to toxic financial instruments or to a bubble in the construction market. However, its financial system is market-based and about 80 % is owned by foreign, mainly EU, banks (Heritage 2012; Inotai 2010). Most investments in the real economy have been financed not only by foreign-owned banks but also by money borrowed on the international financial market (Inotai 2010).

Exacerbated by the falling economy in Europe, Hungary has suffered the worst consequences of the global financial crisis among all Eastern and Central European countries (Bocian and Sadowski 2008; Horvath 2009). The Hungarian government did not take advantage of the high-growth years to implement budgetary reforms; rather, expenditures such as support for social welfare programs and high wage increases in the overstaffed public administration put additional burdens on public expenditures. As a result, the budget deficit in October 2006 reached 9.2 % of the GDP and required the immediate introduction of an austerity program (Inotai 2010).

Due to its huge foreign debt owed by the state, companies and citizens alike, when the global financial crisis broke in late 2008, Hungary was in a very precarious economic situation even though the government had introduced major budget cuts from 2006 to 2008 (Bocian and Sadowski 2008; Draper et al. 2009; Heritage 2012). Although the government had managed to reduce the deficit from 9.3 % of GDP in 2006 to 3.4 % of GDP in 2008, the public debt was still significant, reaching nearly 65 % of the GDP in 2008 (Bocian and Sadowski 2008).

In September 2008, its currency devalued by nearly 13 % against the Euro and the Budapest stock market indices dropped by nearly 40 % (Bocian and Sadowski 2008). By the end of 2008, Hungarian total external debt reached about 120 % of its GDP, compared to less than 50 % in Poland and 40 % in the Czech Republic (OECD 2010b). Private enterprises and households accounted for 74 % of this (Inotai 2010) and almost 90 % of household loans were taken in foreign currencies (Bocian and Sadowski 2008). In November 2008, the IMF approved a US$15.7 billion loan for Hungary as part of a rescue program designed to ease financial market stress; an additional US$8.4 billion was also forthcoming from the European Union and US$1.3 billion from the World Bank (Dapontas 2011).

In the first 8 months of 2009, private consumption fell by 4.2 % as compared to the same period a year ago, industrial production decreased by more than 20 % mainly due to a sharp 24.5 % decline of exports, and substantial decline of domestic consumption (by 12.7 %) (Inotai 2010). The global economic downturn, declining exports, low domestic consumption, and fixed asset accumulation, dampened by government austerity measures, resulted in an economic contraction of 6.3 % in 2009 (CIA 2012). By March 2009, the Hungarian currency had depreciated by 26 % against the Euro, and then by 66 % against the Swiss franc by November 2011, both relative to September 2008 (Valentinyi 2012). Official unemployment grew rapidly, exceeding 10 % in October 2009 (Inotai 2010).

The Hungarian government acted immediately to mitigate the impact of the crisis. Unlimited guarantees for bank deposits were introduced in mid-October 2008 (Bocian and Sadowski 2008). In November 2009, Hungary announced plans for a US$6.9 billion (1.4 trillion forint), two-year stimulus package (Reuters 2009). The rescue package put together by the IMF, European Central Bank, and World Bank worth over US$25 billion, which supported the measures to avert the most dramatic scenario (CIA 2012; Inotai 2010). As a result, Hungary avoided a major banking crisis by making use of the IMF stand-by agreement fund to repurchase the matured bonds and to partially recapitalize the Hungarian Development Bank (Inotai 2010). In addition, the Hungarian National Bank introduced a six-month swap tender in the amount of €5 billion, of which the domestic banking sector readily applied for a sum of €3 billion (Inotai 2010).

The most important Hungarian government measures included value added tax (VAT) increase to 18–25 % range, a 5–6 % increase of excise duties (mainly alcoholic drinks and tobacco), the introduction of a property tax, the domestic taxation of income, and property transferred into different tax shelters (Inotai 2010; Reuters 2009). In the public sector, nominal gross wages have been frozen for 2 years, the traditional one month basic salary bonus was abolished, and the monthly wage of government members was reduced by 15 % (Inotai 2010). In addition, costs connected with memberships in boards of directors or supervisory boards of state-owned firms were reduced by 50 % (Inotai 2010). The largest cuts are in social welfare expenditures US$733 million (156 billion forint) and education US$613 million (130 billion forint) (Inotai 2010). Other measures include the 4 + 1 formula (4 days of work and one day of training in a week) to save about 50,000 jobs, which was launched in May 2009 (Inotai 2010). Special attention was paid to small- and medium-sized companies (SMEs) by allocating US$4.3 billion (€3.2 billion) for credit support and for enterprise development (Bocian and Sadowski 2008; Inotai 2010). For other stabilization programs, please refer to Appendix 1 for the details.

With joint efforts from the Hungarian government, the IMF and the EU, a full-fledged currency and financial crisis was avoided. However, Hungary faced hard times and manifested itself in a substantial negative growth of GDP (26.5 % in 2009) and declining creditworthiness (Terazi and Senel 2011). Fitch Ratings and others downgraded Hungary several times. At the end of March 2009, Standard and Poor's lowered credit rating of Hungary dropped to 'BBB minus' from 'BBB'. This was a bad signal for the owners of new funds that had been attracted to Hungary to help in the process of convergence toward the Euro zone (Magas 2010).

Poland

Poland has pursued economic liberalization since 1990 and stands out as a success story among transition economies. Between 2000 and 2008, its average annual economic growth surpassed 4 % (World Bank, n.d.). During the same period, exports of goods and services grew by 11 % per annum. A booming economy together with European integration reduced the unemployment rate from 20 % in 2002 to 7 % in 2008 and the average annual inflation rate dropped from nearly 30 % in 1991–1999 to 3.4 % in the first decade of the 2000s (World Bank, n.d.). Poland escaped the global economic downturn largely unscathed and was the only country in Europe to escape recession with positive GDP growth in 2009 due to its sound fundamentals (CIA 2012; EU-27 Watch 2012; Heritage 2012). Growth averaged at 3.5 % during the crisis, the highest in Central Europe, and Polish banks continued to record sound profits (World Bank, n.d.).

Poland's interdependence on its EU neighbors (with 79.7 % of the total Polish export in 2009) quickly slowed its growth when the financial crisis hit (Piatkowska 2010). In the second half of 2008, its economy started to experience the negative effects when its growth rate slowed down to 5.2 % and 3.2 % in the third and fourth quarters of 2008, respectively (compared with approximately 6 % in the first half).

On November 30 that year, the government introduced The Stabilization and Development Plan amounting to US$33.7 billion (91.3 billion zloty) (EU-27 Watch 2012; Reichardt 2011). An anti-crisis plan worth about 0.7 % of its GDP was implemented, including such measures as the co-financing of front-loaded investments related to EU funds (OECD 2010c).

Main actions included maintaining the stability of public finances and financial systems, increasing guarantees for banks, creating additional credit schemes for SMEs with the value of US$7.4 billion (20 billion zloty), accelerating the investments financed with EU structural funds estimated at US$6.2 billion (16.8 billion zloty), and the Social Solidarity Reserve of US$420 million (1.14 billion zloty) (EU-27 Watch 2012). The plan also delineated a reduction in general budget spending by US$627 million (1.7 billion zloty) to allow flexibility in the movement of resources (Reichardt 2011). To prevent the economic crisis from further damaging public sector financing, the areas of focus also include inflation control, across-the-board budget and program cuts, raising the national VAT tax, public employment and pension reform, and also fiscal consolidation and public finance at the local level (Reichardt 2011). Like all other EU countries, Poland's public debt has increased to dangerous levels and the budget deficit remains high, partially due to loss of revenues (Reichardt 2011).

Polish dependency on loans in foreign currency was relatively low. Poland was one of the region's first to regulate lending in foreign currencies. Banks were advised to require higher credit worthiness for residential credits denominated in foreign currencies than for loans in local currency. With the sight of the financial crisis, Polish authorities encouraged banks to hold an additional 2 % of risk-weighted capital above the Basel II requirements, thus retain their profits for 2008 (OECD 2010c; World Bank, n.d.). During the crisis, banks were obliged to report their new exposure to foreign entities on a daily basis (World Bank, n.d.). The National Bank of Poland bonds was repurchased in advance to increase market liquidity. In addition, crisis coping financial actions were coordinated by the dedicated Financial Stability Committee (Plociennik 2012). Guarantees for individual deposits were also raised to reassure depositors (OECD 2010c).

For FDI, after the record year 2007 in receiving €16.7 billion, the amount was reduced to €10.0 billion in 2008 and €8.3 billion in 2009 (Piatkowska 2010). In 2009, exports amounted to €98.3 billion, demonstrating a decline by 15.5 % (Piatkowska 2010). Public debt rose to 50 % of the GDP (Piatkowska 2010). However, in the last quarter of 2009, the economic growth accelerated to 3.0 %, and the growth of GDP amounted to 1.8 % over 2009 (Piatkowska 2010). Although the Polish economy is open, it remains relatively independent on the foreign trade (40 %). A safe haven for the Polish business is its relatively large and conservative internal market, divided into smaller local markets, with a high share of labor-consuming services (Plociennik 2012). Another important reason was the Flexible Credit Line granted by the IMF, with its stabilizing effect on the market rating of Poland (Plociennik 2012).

The main reasons that safeguard Poland's economy from drastic downturn include: first, the Polish economy is much more closed compared to the other member states; second, with currency freedom the Polish government used a strong depreciation against the Euro to increase its competitiveness; third, the inflow of EU funds and their own investment focused recovery plan cushioned the underutilization of production capacities and tightening of credit conditions; fourth, the private consumption was maintained by fiscal support for households; and fifth, the conservative regulatory policy and sound balance sheets of the Polish banks preserved them from high losses (EU-27 Watch 2012).

Romania

Romania began the transition from Communism in 1989 and emerged in 2000 from a three-year recession (CIA 2012). GDP growth averaged over 6.5 % per year from 2003 to 2008 and reached 15.7 % of the GDP in the first quarter of 2008, mainly due to foreign direct investment, capital inflows and domestic consumption (CIA 2012; IMF 2009; Voinea et al. 2010). However, inflation rose in 2007–2008, driven in part by strong consumer demand and high wage growth, rising energy costs, a nation-wide drought affecting food prices, and a relaxation of fiscal discipline (CIA 2012).

The easy foreign capital fueled consumer spending and led to an investment boom by local companies, yet with high exposure to international financial shock as well. In Romania, much of the consumption was financed by private sector debt and most of it in foreign currency (IMF 2009). In addition, strong wage raise, an increased volume of remittances and a rapid expansion of nongovernmental domestic credit pushed private consumption on an unsustainable path, leading to an overheated economy (Voinea et al. 2010). Increasing inflows of foreign capital, driven by high interest rates and potential gains in the property market, led to a continuous appreciation of the domestic currency, the ron. This, in turn led to an acceleration of imports, which rose faster than exports, widening the current account deficit to −12.3 % at the end of 2008. Also, fiscal policy was pro-cyclical, with the budget deficit rising from −0.8 % in 2005 to −5.4 % of GDP at the end of 2008, mainly due to substantially higher than planned current spending in public wages and social transfers (Voinea et al. 2010).

Romanian trade dependence on the EU market has been increased from around 30 % in 1989 to 70 % and Greek banks own 12 % of Romanian banking system (Voinea et al. 2010). With the global downturn in financial markets and trade, Romania's GDP contracted markedly in the last quarter of 2008 (CIA 2012; Heritage 2012; IMF 2009). The effects of the worldwide slump have also been aggravated by economic weaknesses within Romania itself (IMF 2009). Romania's GDP fell more than 7 % in 2009, prompting the government to seek a US$26 billion (€20 billion) emergency assistance package from the IMF, the EU, and other international lenders (CIA 2012). On May 4, 2009 the IMF's Executive Board approved a 24-month Stand-By Arrangement in the amount of US$17.1 billion (€12.95 billion) (IMF 2009). Attached with the package requires the Romanian government to push through austerity measures, including cutting its budget deficit to 3 % (Ban 2010).

When the global credit crunched, capital from abroad suddenly dropped and spilled over into the exchange rate. From October 2008 to May 2009, Romanian currency has depreciated by more than 15 % against the Euro (IMF 2009). Although the National Bank of Romania has allocated US$642 million (2 billion ron) to resolve the problems when the crisis hit (Bocian and Sadowski 2008), unfortunately the government ran increasingly large fiscal deficits during the good times, leaving little room to maneuver when the economy turned down (IMF 2009).

During the first 3 months of 2009, Romanian companies survived to a certain extent, based on the accrual of previous years and on contracts in progress. Starting from April, the economic environment became more hostile. Exports crushed due to dramatic decrease of demand in the EU area, fiscal pressure increased, interest rates remained high, and domestic consumer demand dropped off a lot faster than estimated (Sbughea 2011). Largely, Romanian macroeconomic was kept under control with its national currency to some extent stabilized, after a depreciation of approximately 15 %. The IMF package discouraged potential speculative attacks on the Romanian currency, and inflation in 2009 did not accelerate its raising (Sbughea 2011).

Romanian government made significant changes to its tax legislation at the end of 2008 and in early 2009 in order to offset the impact of the global financial crisis. Changes include exempting capital gains realized by companies and individuals in 2009 from share trading on the Romanian Stock Exchange. From January 1, 2009, the government abolished taxation on interest derived from deposits and other saving instruments (previously, interest on term deposits was taxable at 16 %) (QFinance 2010b). IT programmers would continue to be exempted from income tax in 2009 to encourage the development of the IT industry (QFinance 2010b). It also introduced a tax exemption in respect of dividends reinvested for the purpose of maintaining or increasing employee numbers (QFinance 2010b). The exemption also applied to dividends reinvested in the share capital of another legal entity.

In 2009, the Romanian economy experienced one of the sharpest contractions in its recent history. The net exports adjusted sharply, contracting from around 15 % of the GDP in 2007 to a little over 5 % of the GDP at the end of 2009 (Voinea et al. 2010). In 2009, private consumption dived by 9.2 % year-on-year as the shock to real incomes influenced household purchasing patterns (Voinea et al. 2010). The IMF financial package approved in May 2009 was to be used for fiscal consolidation, banking reform, and reducing inflation to help restore financial stability. The fiscal reforms include measures to improve budgeting, streamline public wages and pensions, and make public enterprises more efficient to ensure that the deficit will remain low in the future. These reforms helped produce a leaner, more efficient and more transparent public sector (IMF 2009). In addition, banks have agreed to provide additional capital as a cushion against future losses, and foreign banks in Romania have agreed to keep their money in the country (IMF 2009).

However, the political crisis that led to the parliament dismissing the government in October 2009 resulted in the freezing of the bailout package (Ban 2010). In 2010, two of the three main international credit rating agencies, Standard & Poor's and Fitch, downgraded the country's rating to junk status (Voinea et al. 2010).

Chapter 3
National Intellectual Capital Development of the Five Emerging European Countries

In this chapter, we first present the development of national intellectual capital in these five emerging European countries over six years, and then graphically display the relationship between each individual capital with GDP per capita (ppp). Afterwards, we describe the relative position of long-term and short-term intellectual capital and explain the dynamics of national intellectual capital for three time periods (2005–2006, 2007–2008, and 2009–2010). Finally, we illustrate the NIC trajectory of these five countries on three-dimensional (3D) 48-country landscapes.

National Intellectual Capital Development

The national intellectual capital measurement model in this study is based on the indicators described in Appendix 3, containing human capital, market capital, process capital, renewal capital, and financial capital. This model has been statistically validated for its validity and reliability, and the definitions of the indicators are listed in Appendix 4. This booklet series covers a total of 48 countries in 11 country clusters (see Appendix 5 for details).

For a full picture of all 48 countries being studied, Appendix 6 exhibits the scores and rankings of human capital, market capital, process capital, renewal capital, financial capital, and overall national intellectual capital (hereafter termed NIC) covered in this booklet series. Table 3.1 summarizes the status of the five emerging European countries compared to the total 48 countries reported in Appendix 6. Appendix 7 provides the individual country profiles with additional statistics. For the NIC ranking, the Czech Republic ranks 25, followed by Hungary at 29, Poland at 32, Bulgaria at 35, and Romania at 39.

The following six figures compare human capital, market capital, process capital, renewal capital, financial capital, and NIC of the five countries. All individual capital scores are based on a scale from 1 to 10 with the NIC score being the sum of the five capital scores.

C. Y.-Y. Lin et al., *National Intellectual Capital and the Financial Crisis in Bulgaria, Czech Republic, Hungary, Romania, and Poland*, SpringerBriefs in Economics,
DOI: 10.1007/978-1-4614-8018-1_3,

Table 3.1 National intellectual capital ranking of Bulgaria, the Czech Republic, Hungary, Poland, and Romania (2005–2010)

Country	Human capital		Market capital		Process capital		Renewal capital		Financial capital		NIC	
	Score	Ranking	Score	Ranking	Score	Ranking	Score	Ranking	Score	Ranking	Score	Ranking
Bulgaria	5.493	34	4.929	31	4.054	36	1.589	41	8.646	37	24.710	35
The Czech Republic	5.995	30	5.720	18	5.378	25	2.905	24	9.271	27	29.269	25
Hungary	6.674	24	4.836	32	5.095	29	2.301	29	9.046	29	27.952	29
Poland	6.393	29	4.246	41	3.895	38	1.819	35	8.945	30	25.299	32
Romania	5.829	32	4.219	42	3.806	39	1.685	38	8.594	39	24.133	39

Human Capital

National human capital mainly represents a nation's investment in nurturing qualified human resources, such as higher education enrollment, skilled labor, and public expenditure on education. It is a long-term oriented NIC (Lin and Edvinsson 2011: 323), taking time to develop yet not susceptible to external impact. Figure 3.1 shows that human capital of these five countries was relatively stable over the studied six years, with Bulgaria having a slight human capital decline in 2010 compared to 2005. The other four countries had increases in human capital over the six years.

Market Capital

National market capital mainly represents international trade and relationships, such as cross-border ventures, globalization, and exports of goods. Figure 3.2 shows that other than Poland all the countries had market capital decrease in 2008, with Romania having the greatest dip. In 2010, market capital of these countries bounced back to 2005 levels or surpassing it, except the Czech Republic and Hungary. Hungary started off with the second highest market capital in 2005, yet slid to the lowest in this country cluster. Poland, being the laggard in 2005, has continuous market capital increases over the years and has the third highest score in 2010.

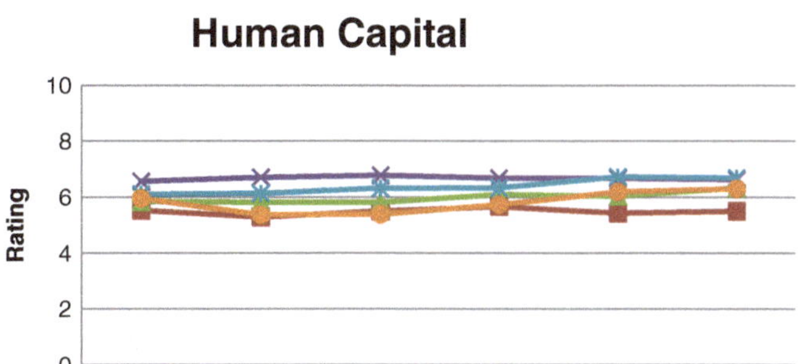

	2005	2006	2007	2008	2009	2010
Bulgaria	5.54	5.30	5.50	5.67	5.44	5.51
Czech Republic	5.85	5.82	5.81	6.10	6.04	6.34
Hungary	6.56	6.71	6.77	6.68	6.68	6.64
Poland	6.11	6.15	6.32	6.34	6.74	6.69
Romania	5.96	5.38	5.39	5.74	6.20	6.31

Fig. 3.1 Human capital of Bulgaria, the Czech Republic, Hungary, Poland, and Romania

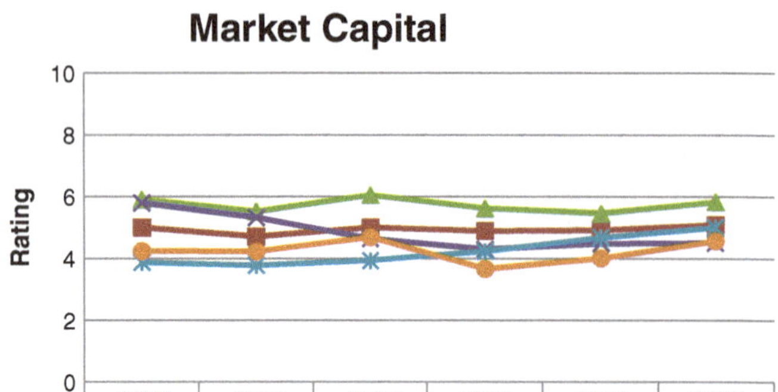

	2005	2006	2007	2008	2009	2010
Bulgaria	4.99	4.70	4.99	4.89	4.92	5.08
Czech Republic	5.90	5.51	6.04	5.61	5.45	5.82
Hungary	5.79	5.31	4.64	4.30	4.48	4.50
Poland	3.87	3.78	3.93	4.23	4.68	4.99
Romania	4.22	4.21	4.67	3.65	4.00	4.55

Fig. 3.2 Market capital of Bulgaria, the Czech Republic, Hungary, Poland, and Romania

Process Capital

National process capital represents the infrastructure required for building a prosperous society, such as capital availability, mobile phone subscribers, and government efficiency. Figure 3.3 shows a clear two clusters in 2005, with the Czech Republic and Hungary in the high cluster and the other three countries in the low cluster with Poland having the lowest score. In 2010, the Czech Republic and Hungary are still in the high cluster, yet the gap with the low cluster reduced. That is, the former two countries had process capital decrease, whereas the latter three countries advanced their process capital, with Poland and Romania having a continuous improvement after 2008.

Renewal Capital

National renewal capital represents the capability of R&D and innovation, such as R&D spending, scientific articles, and patents. Figure 3.4 shows that the Czech Republic and Hungary consistently had the first and the second highest renewal capital scores over the years. When compared with 2005, the renewal capital of Bulgaria decreased, the Czech Republic increased, Hungary decreased, Poland stayed almost the same, and Romania had some increase in 2010.

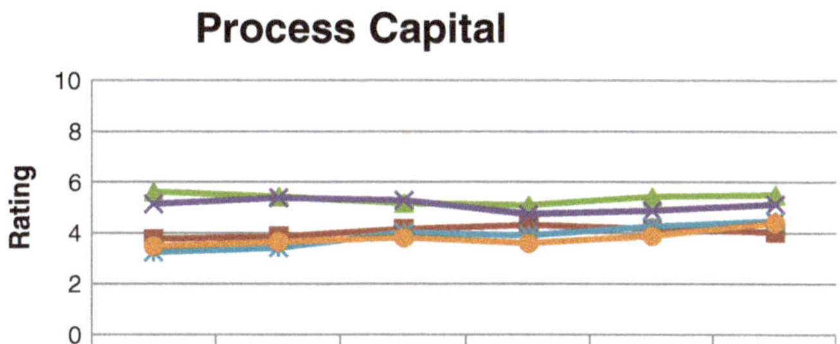

	2005	2006	2007	2008	2009	2010
Bulgaria	3.76	3.87	4.16	4.32	4.17	4.04
Czech Republic	5.63	5.43	5.18	5.09	5.43	5.50
Hungary	5.15	5.38	5.29	4.73	4.88	5.13
Poland	3.26	3.43	4.02	3.92	4.27	4.48
Romania	3.48	3.65	3.82	3.60	3.89	4.40

Fig. 3.3 Process capital of Bulgaria, the Czech Republic, Hungary, Poland, and Romania

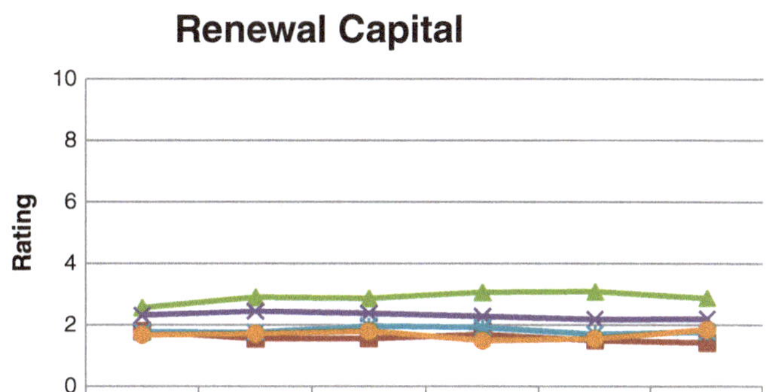

	2005	2006	2007	2008	2009	2010
Bulgaria	1.79	1.56	1.56	1.69	1.50	1.42
Czech Republic	2.58	2.92	2.88	3.07	3.10	2.89
Hungary	2.31	2.46	2.38	2.28	2.18	2.19
Poland	1.77	1.77	1.97	1.92	1.70	1.78
Romania	1.68	1.72	1.80	1.50	1.56	1.85

Fig. 3.4 Renewal capital of Bulgaria, the Czech Republic, Hungary, Poland, and Romania

Financial Capital

National financial capital is the GDP per capita (ppp) in US dollars converted to a score between 1–10. The score transformation process is explained in Appendix 3. Figure 3.5 shows Romania had the lowest financial capital and Hungary had a little financial capital decrease over the years. Yet in real dollars, the average GDP per capita (ppp) from 2005 to 2010 was US$11,955 for Bulgaria, US$23,514 for the Czech Republic, US$18,385 for Hungary, US$16,574 for Poland, and US$11,299 for Romania.

NIC

NIC is the overall national intellectual capital containing the five types of capital discussed above. Figure 3.6 presents NIC trends and shows two clear clusters in 2005. The Czech Republic and Hungary are in the high cluster and the other three countries in the low cluster. The former two countries remained having the first and second NIC score in 2010. The Czech Republic was relatively stable in NIC over the years. Hungary had a relatively large scale NIC slide; on the contrary, Poland had a continuous NIC progress and narrowed the gap between the two countries. The NIC status change of Hungary and Poland largely reflects the economic up and down of these two countries during this period. In the outburst of 2008 financial crisis, Bulgaria had a slight NIC increase, whereas Romania had a decrease.

The Relationship Between Each Individual Capital and GDP Per Capita (ppp)

We investigate the relationship between each individual capital and economic growth by using the following six figures (Figs. 3.7, 3.8, 3.9, 3.10, 3.11, 3.12). The graphs have four dimensions: the *x* axis changes from graph to graph (NIC, human capital, market capital, process capital, and renewal capital), the *y* axis is a fixed dimension of GDP per capita (ppp) in US dollars (hereafter termed GDP), the color shade represents renewal capital with red denoting higher levels of renewal capital, and the bubble size denoting the population of a nation. Figure 3.7 is the relationship between NIC and GDP for all 48 countries. Figures 3.8, 3.9, 3.10, 3.11, 3.12 display the co-development of the intellectual capital-GDP relationship over the six-year timeframe for the five countries. Since financial capital is the 1–10 score converted from the GDP, there is no need to plot its relationship with GDP in US dollars. In the figures, 2005 is the starting point tagged with the name of the countries, and the ending point is 2010.

Figure 3.7 is particularly plotted to clearly show a full picture of the relationship between NIC and GDP for 48 countries in 2010. The strong positive correlation indicates that the higher the NIC the higher the GDP, and vice versa. Consequently, enhancing NIC is definitely a strategic issue that deserves the attention of national policy makers.

With the status of all 48 countries as the background, Figure 3.8 indicates that NIC and GDP co-development of the five countries falls within the middle and

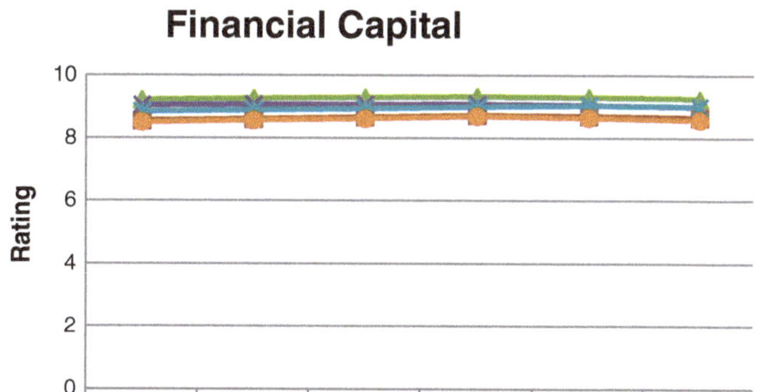

	2005	2006	2007	2008	2009	2010
Bulgaria	8.55	8.60	8.66	8.72	8.70	8.65
Czech Republic	9.21	9.26	9.30	9.32	9.29	9.25
Hungary	9.04	9.07	9.06	9.08	9.04	8.99
Poland	8.84	8.88	8.94	8.99	9.03	9.00
Romania	8.50	8.56	8.61	8.68	8.64	8.57

Fig. 3.5 Financial capital of Bulgaria, Czech Republic, Hungary, Poland, and Romania

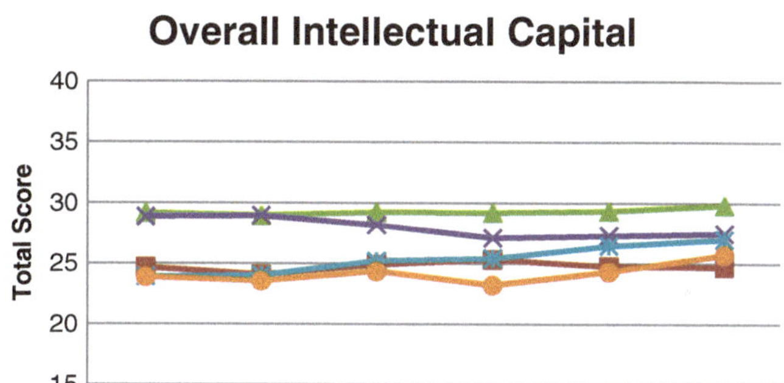

	2005	2006	2007	2008	2009	2010
Bulgaria	24.64	24.03	24.88	25.30	24.73	24.69
Czech Republic	29.16	28.94	29.21	29.19	29.32	29.80
Hungary	28.86	28.93	28.15	27.07	27.26	27.44
Poland	23.85	24.01	25.17	25.39	26.42	26.95
Romania	23.84	23.52	24.30	23.17	24.28	25.68

Fig. 3.6 NIC of Bulgaria, the Czech Republic, Hungary, Poland, and Romania

middle-lower range of the 48 countries continuum. For Bulgaria and Romania, their developments are intertwined. In general, they had similar levels of NIC development which correlated to GDP growth. However, Bulgaria regressed whereas Romania advanced NIC after the financial crisis. The Czech Republic has the highest NIC and good GDP growth over the six years. Hungary and Poland

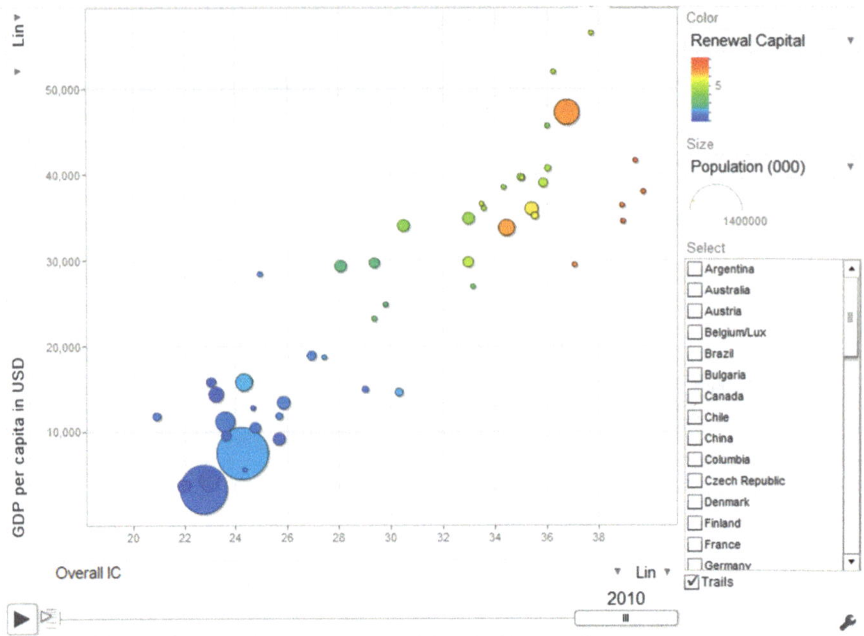

Fig. 3.7 NIC versus GDP per capita (ppp) for 48 countries in 2010

started off with wide apart NIC-GDP level, with Poland at the lower and Hungary at the middle part of the graph. Over the six years, Hungary's relatively large scale decline and Poland' continuous improvement narrowed their NIC-GDP gap year by year to the point of becoming similar in 2010. This phenomenon truly reflects their national development during the financial crisis years, Hungary with large public debt had to launch consolidation started 2004 and Poland is known as the champion in the emerging European region.

Figure 3.9 shows that the co-development of human capital and GDP of the five countries is at the middle range among the 48 countries. The development pattern is somewhat similar to that shown in Figure 3.8 for NIC. The human capital-GDP co-developments of Bulgaria and Romania are intertwined; however Bulgaria's human capital declined and that of Romania increased after the financial crisis. Surprisingly as a Stage 3 innovation driven country, the Czech Republic's human capital lagged behind most of the other countries except Bulgaria in 2010. Hungary was ahead of Poland in human capital in 2005. Over six years development, Poland has caught up with and surpassed Hungary a little in human capital in 2010.

In general, the bubble formation of Figure 3.10 is very different from that of other figures in this section, without a clear belt shape continuum from the bottom left to the upper right. It means that market capital is not as highly correlated with GDP as the other capitals are in this set of data. A further explanation is that market capital of advanced countries (generally positioned at the upper right) is

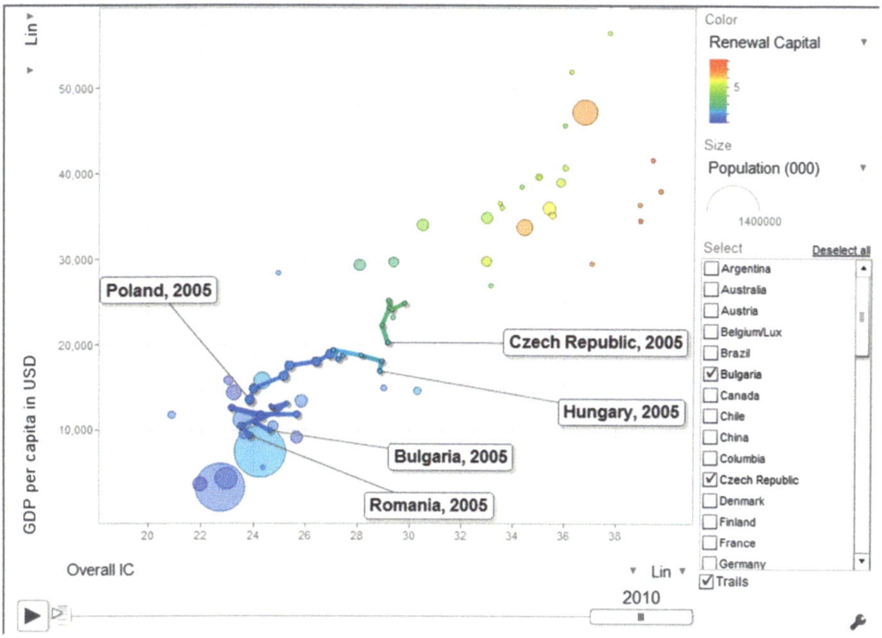

Fig. 3.8 The development of NIC and GDP per capita (ppp) for the five emerging European countries from 2005 to 2010

not necessarily better than that of emerging countries (the two big bubbles at the bottom center are China and India).

Development of the five emerging European countries is located in the lower middle section of the graph. That is, their market capital is relatively good yet GDP is comparatively low. This figure indicates that most of the countries experienced declining market capital over the six years period, except Poland. Bulgaria had an early 2006 market capital decline, rebounded in 2007, then declined again in 2008 with small scale variation afterwards. The Czech Republic had a similar development pattern as that of Bulgaria, yet with the highest market capital and GDP score in this country cluster. Again, Hungary and Poland started off with wide apart market capital level. Over years, Hungary's relatively large scale decline and Poland' continuous improvement not only narrowed their market capital-GDP gap but Poland also surpassed Hungary in market capital in 2010. This finding partially supports Poland's weathering through this financial crisis successfully as the only country with a positive GDP growth in 2009 in the emerging European region. Romania's market capital dropped drastically in 2008, yet rebounded in 2009 with continuous improvement afterwards.

In Figure 3.11, the belt shape continuum appears again, indicating that process capital is highly related with GDP in general. The process capital-GDP co-development of the Czech Republic and Hungary is in the middle range among the

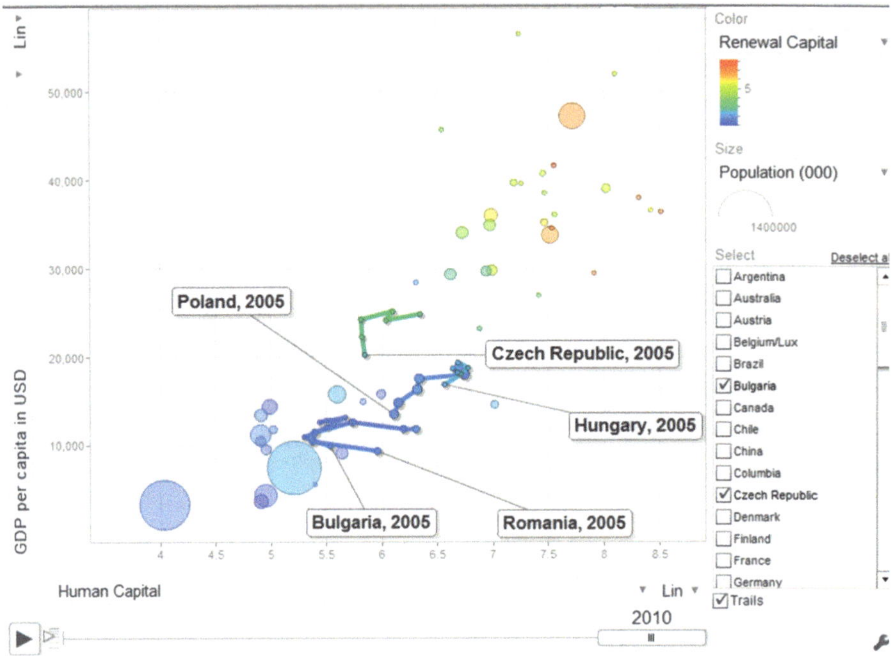

Fig. 3.9 The development of human capital and GDP per capita (ppp) for the five emerging European countries from 2005 to 2010

48 countries; those of the other three countries are at the lower part of the continuum. Bulgaria had a late process capital decline started 2009. The Czech Republic had an early decline in 2006 and began rebounding in 2009, accompanied with some GDP growth. Hungary experienced a continuous process capital decline in 2007 but rebounded in 2009, yet without much GDP growth. Poland had a little set back in process capital in 2008, however rebounded in 2009 with a little GDP growth. Unlike previous graphs, although the gap between Hungary and Poland narrowed as well, Poland's process capital-GDP still lagged behind that of Hungary's in 2010. Romania's process capital declined in 2008, yet it rebounded strongly and surpassed that of Bulgaria's in 2010.

Figure 3.12 indicates that renewal capital and GDP co-development of the 48 countries had two formations. The spreading formation for the advanced countries in the upper right, and the belt shape continuum for the less developed countries in the bottom left. This means, for advanced countries, higher renewal capital does not necessarily correspond to higher GDP. Yet, for less developed countries, increases in renewal capital correlate closely with GDP growth. From the formation of the bottom left continuum, it is clear that small increases in renewal capital were accompanied by relatively high GDP growth. This finding reveals a strong message that investing in renewal capital development may benefit GDP growth for developing countries.

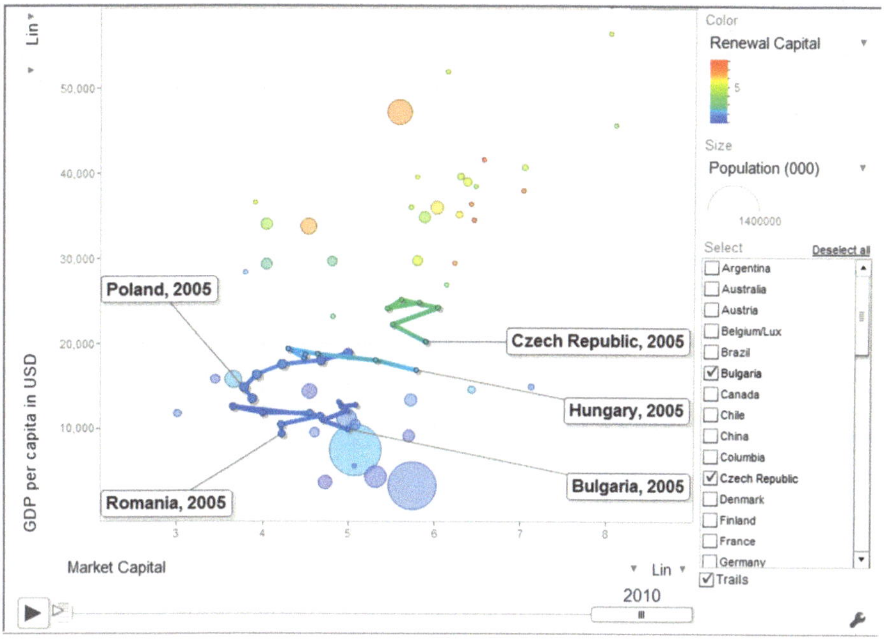

Fig. 3.10 The development of market capital and GDP per capita (ppp) for the five emerging European countries from 2005 to 2010

The renewal capital and GDP co-development of the five countries is at the middle to lower range of the 48 countries. Again, the developments of Bulgaria and Romania were intertwined, Bulgaria's renewal capital declined whereas that of Romania improved after the financial crisis. The Czech Republic had relatively good renewal capital progress until its decline in 2010. Hungary had a continuous renewal capital decline over the years. Poland did not have renewal capital progress over the years and still lagged behind Hungary in 2010. As the champion in the emerging European region, Poland's weakest renewal capital may be the focus of its next development stage.

Long-Term and Short-Term National Intellectual Capital

In addition to the above six figures that show the relationship of each individual capital with GDP, Figs. 3.13, 3.14, 3.15, 3.16 further plot the relationships between human capital and renewal capital, as well as between market capital and process capital. In our first study (Lin and Edvinsson 2011: 324), we found that the combined increase in human capital and renewal capital would lead to a nation's long term development; whereas the combined increase in market capital and

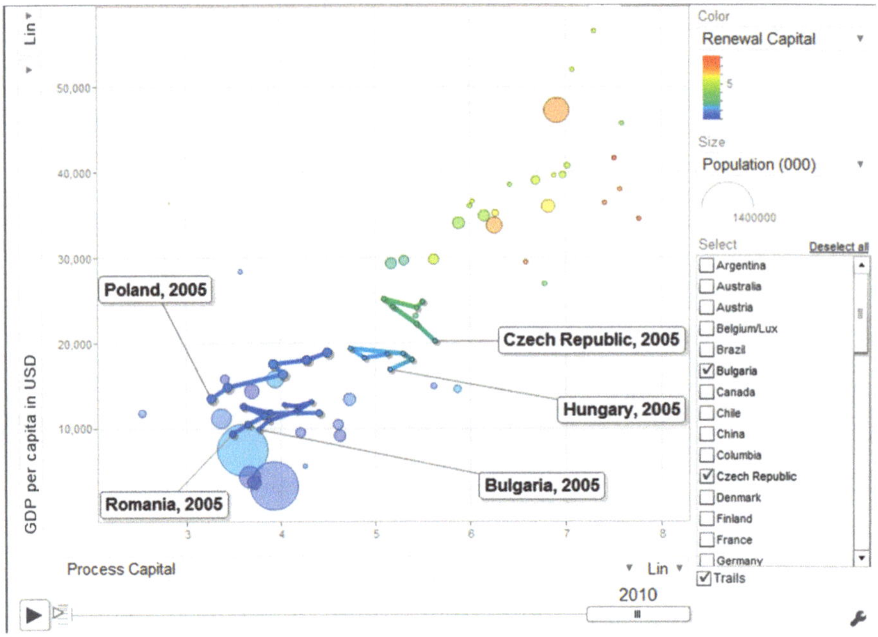

Fig. 3.11 The development of process capital and GDP per capita (ppp) for the five emerging European countries from 2005 to 2010

process capital might result in more immediate economic development. To present their relationships, Figs. 3.13, 3.14, 3.15, 3.16 map the four capitals on a coordinate with two types of presentation. Based on the same data, Figs. 3.13 and 3.15 exhibit the scatter plot for the five countries only, whereas Figs. 3.14 and 3.16 show all the 48 countries as background so that readers will know the relative positions of these five countries. Please note that the connotation of color shade for Figs. 3.14 and 3.16 has been changed from renewal capital to GDP per capita (ppp).

Both Figs. 3.13 and 3.14 indicate that Bulgaria had both human capital and renewal capital declined in 2006, rebounded in 2007 and 2008, then declined again after 2009. The country has the lowest long-term NIC in this country cluster. The Czech Republic had some progress in its long-term NIC over the years, with the highest renewal capital in this country cluster. However, its 2010 human capital is still behind that of Hungary and Poland and deserves some attention. Hungary slid in both human capital and renewal capital from 2008, which may indicate its weakened long-term development prospect. Poland had long-term NIC improvement until 2008; its human capital had a continuous progress yet renewal capital decline in 2009. Romania had a clear human capital drop in 2006, and then rebounded in 2008 with a human capital increase yet renewal capital decrease. In 2010, Romania had both human capital and renewal capital progress.

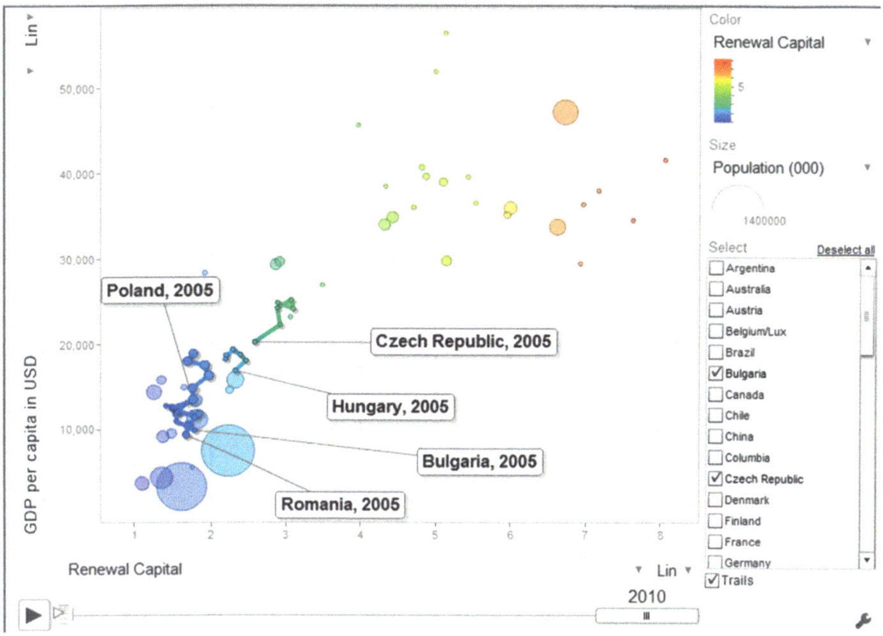

Fig. 3.12 The development of renewal capital and GDP per capita (ppp) for the five emerging European countries from 2005 to 2010

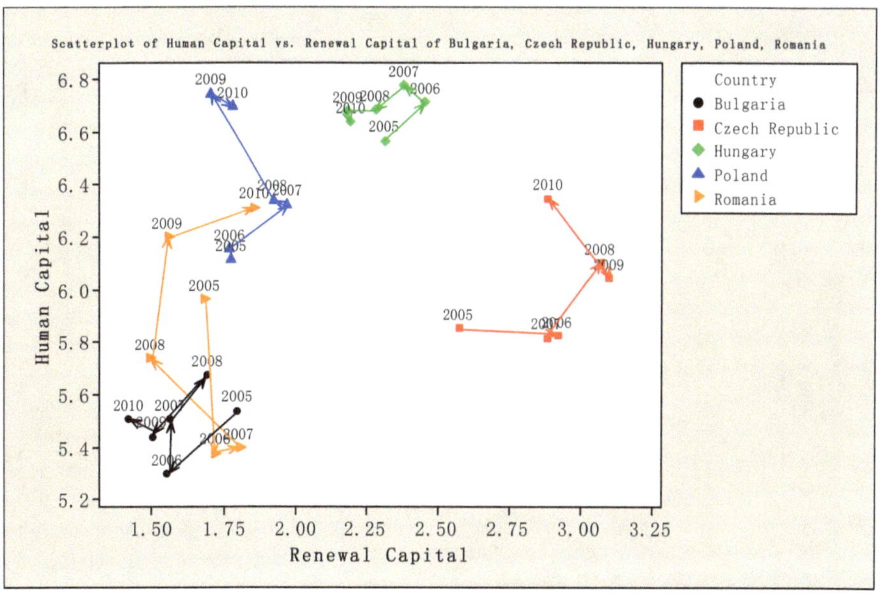

Fig. 3.13 A scatterplot of human capital versus renewal capital of Bulgaria, the Czech Republic, Hungary, Poland, and Romania

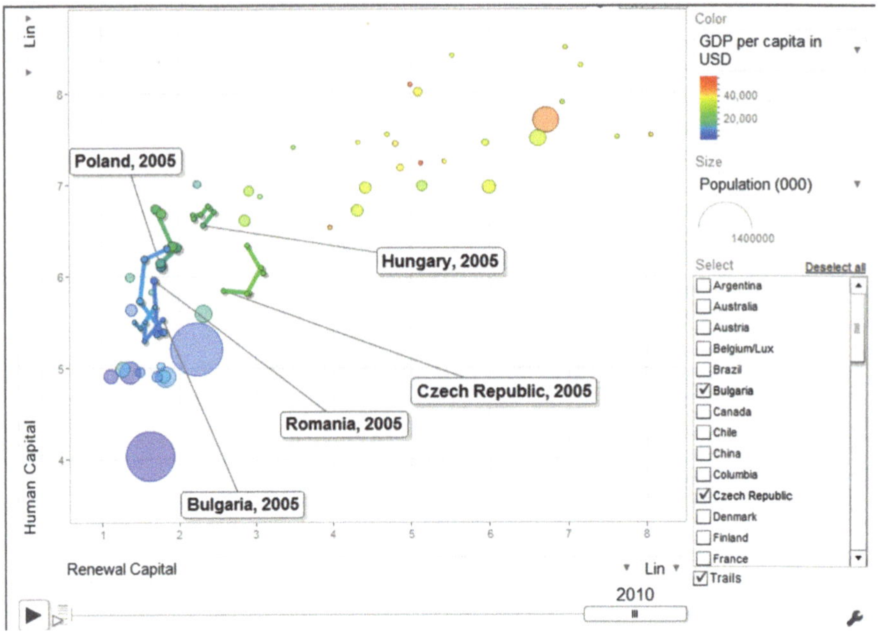

Fig. 3.14 Human capital versus renewal capital of Bulgaria, the Czech Republic, Hungary, Poland, and Romania

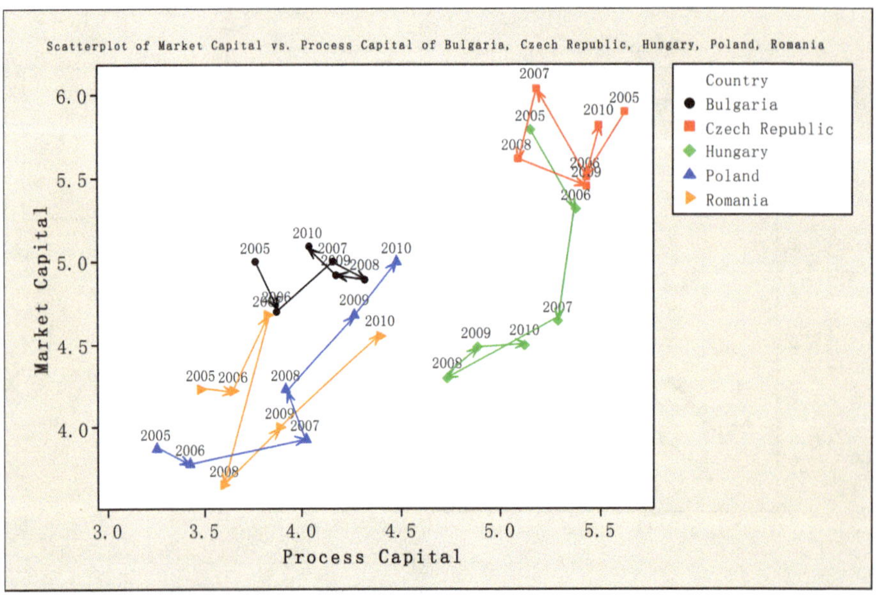

Fig. 3.15 A scatterplot of market capital versus process capital of Bulgaria, the Czech Republic, Hungary, Poland, and Romania

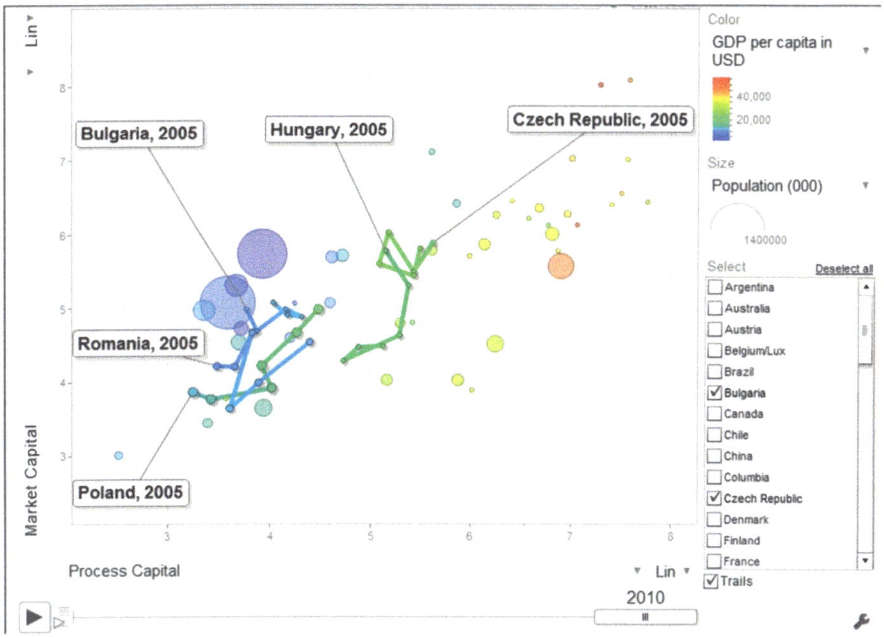

Fig. 3.16 Market capital versus process capital of Bulgaria, the Czech Republic, Hungary, Poland, and Romania

Figure 3.14 indicates that most of these countries are at the middle left part of long-term NIC development among the 48 countries, showing relatively low renewal capital. Bulgaria is low at both human capital and renewal capital, which projects its weakness in future national development. The Czech Republic falls in the middle on this graph. Advancement in its long-term NIC should be a goal of its next stage development. Hungary had relatively small scale changes in its long-term NIC over the years. However, with its slow progression in long-term NIC, countries like Poland will catch it up soon. Poland and Romania are also low in renewal capital on the 48-country landscape.

Figures 3.15 and 3.16 map market capital and process capital of the five countries on a coordinate. Market capital refers to the general assets embodied in a nation's relationship with international markets while process capital refers to the national infrastructure. For short-term competition, these are the two types of capital that can be expected to produce faster results if a nation is willing to engage in more extensive investments.

Figure 3.15 show that Bulgaria had a better starting point in both market capital and process capital than Poland and Romania in 2005. It experienced market capital decline and rebound twice, largely with process capital progress over the six years. However, its process capital lagged behind Poland and Romania in 2010, even though there is internal score improvement. Short-term NIC of the Czech Republic is at the high-high corner of the scatterplot, with decline starting in 2006, however there was a rebound in 2010. In 2005, Hungary started off with a similar level of market capital and was not too far behind in process capital from the Czech Republic. However, Hungary had a relatively large scale decline in market capital in 2006 and a process capital decline in 2007 until they rebounded a little in 2009. In 2010, the short-term NIC gap between Hungary and the Czech Republic widened. Poland experienced a relatively large scale and continuous short-term NIC improvement with a little set back in process capital in 2008 only. Romania had a drastic decline in market capital, yet rebounded strongly in both market capital and process capital.

Figure 3.16 shows that, in a 48-country landscape, short-term NIC of the Czech Republic and Hungary are in the middle and the other three countries are in the lower part of the graph. Particularly, Hungary had the largest scale of both market capital and process capital decline over the years. Bulgaria had process capital decline. The above intangible assets findings are in agreement with the economic development of these five countries during the financial crisis.

Dynamics of National Intellectual Capital in Three Time Periods

The previous illustrations and graphs describe more internal progression or regression of NIC in each country with individual capital score changes over the six years and the path of development of various capitals. The ranking changes to be introduced in this section represent external competitiveness. Ranking, by and large, is a zero-sum game in which the advance of one country simultaneously marks the decline of another.

In order to probe the dynamics of NIC change before and after the financial crisis, we plotted Figs. 3.17, 3.18, 3.19, 3.20, 3.21, 3.22, 3.23, 3.24, 3.25, 3.26 and Table 3.2 in three time periods: 2005–2006, 2007–2008, and 2009–2010. To have a clearer presentation, we separate the data in two sets. The first set contains capital scores and ranking changes of human capital, market capital and process capital in Figs. 3.17, 3.19, 3.21, 3.23, and 3.25. The second set exhibits capital scores and ranking changes of renewal capital, financial capital, and average NIC in Figs. 3.18, 3.20, 3.22, 3.24, and 3.26.

The figures are mapped based on the mean capital scores and ranking changes of each period. Ranking change is next to each capital score and copied from the bold-faced ranking difference of columns 2, 5, 7, and 9 in Table 3.2. To cite an example, for the human capital ranking difference of Bulgaria (−3, 3, −6, −3), the first change "−3" represents the difference between the 3rd (2009–2010) and 1st (2005–2006) period and is plotted at 2005; a ranking change "3" represents the difference between the 2nd period (2007–2008) and 1st (2005–2006) and is plotted at 2007; a ranking change "−6" represents the difference between the 3rd period (2009–2010) and 2nd (2007–2008) and is plotted at 2009; and the last ranking

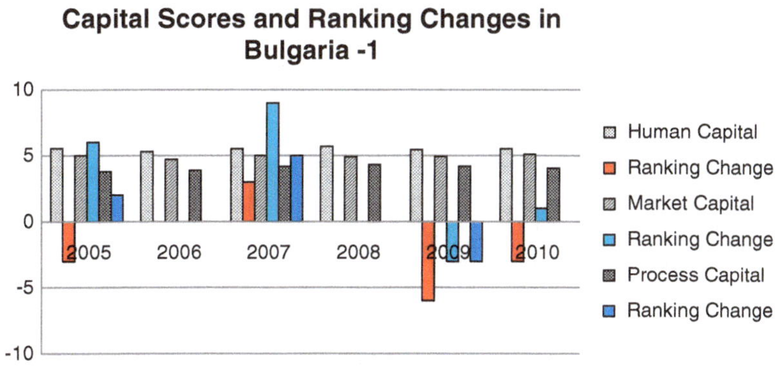

Fig. 3.17 Human capital, market capital, process capital, and ranking changes in Bulgaria

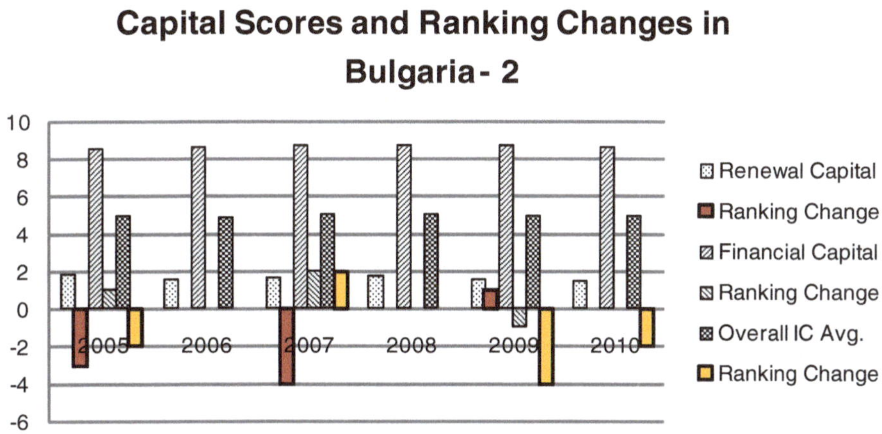

Fig. 3.18 Renewal capital, financial capital, average NIC, and ranking changes in Bulgaria

change "−3" represents the difference between the 3rd period (2009–2010) and 6-year average ranking (exhibited in Table 3.1) and is plotted at 2010. Special attention can be paid to the negative numbers, which mean that the level of a particular capital was higher before than after the financial crisis. Since it is easier to read figures than tables, we will describe the finding of each figure separately.

From Fig. 3.17 and Table 3.2, Bulgaria's human capital ranking changes (−3, 3, −6, −3) indicate that the country was losing international competitiveness in human capital. However, the first and second ranking gains (6, 9, −3, −1) for market capital indicates that Bulgaria was improving international competitiveness in market capital during and after the financial crisis. The third negative number (−3) means its market capital ranking in 2007–2008 is better than that of 2009–2010. The ranking changes (2, 5, −3, 0) of Bulgaria's process capital has the same pattern as that of market capital, only with a smaller scale.

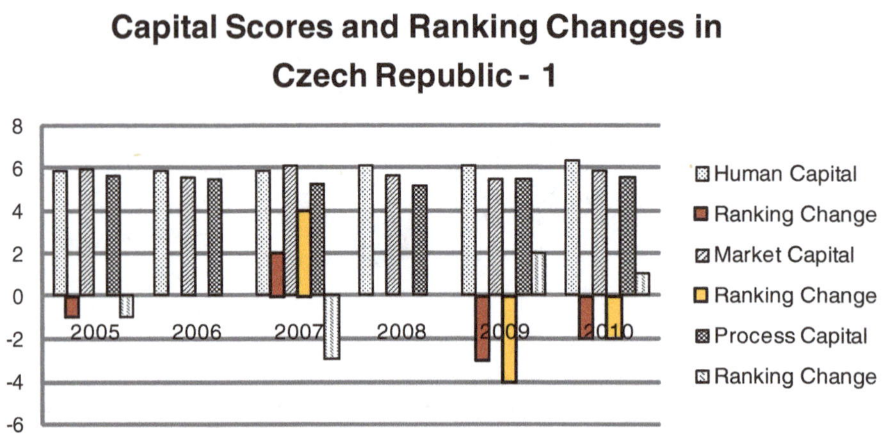

Fig. 3.19 Human capital, market capital, process capital, and ranking changes in the Czech Republic

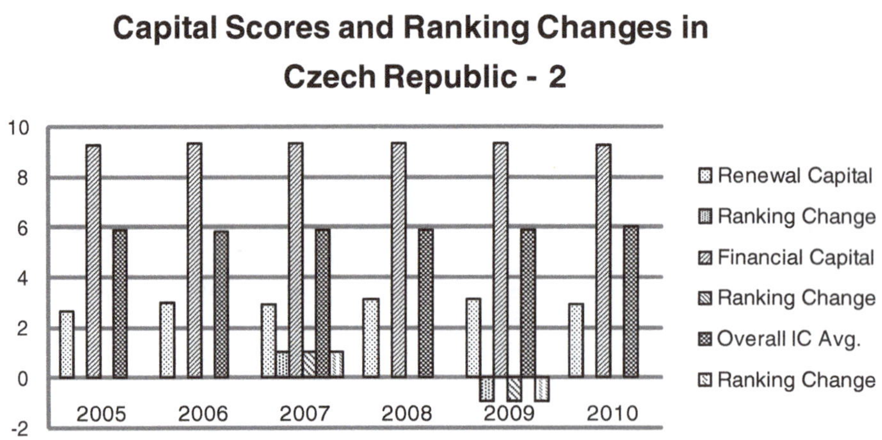

Fig. 3.20 Renewal capital, financial capital, average NIC, and ranking changes in the Czech Republic

Figure 3.18 and Table 3.2 show that the ranking changes of renewal capital (−3, −4, 1, 0), financial capital (1, 2, −1, 0) and average NIC (−2, 2, −4, −2) indicate that Bulgaria was losing renewal capital and NIC international competitiveness after the financial crisis. In general, Bulgaria had ranking progress in market capital and process capital during and after the financial crisis; however, it lost its human capital, renewal capital, and NIC international competitiveness after the crisis.

Figure 3.19 and Table 3.2 show the ranking changes of human capital (−1, 2, −3, −2), market capital (0, 4, −4, −2), and process capital (−1, −3, 2, 1) for the

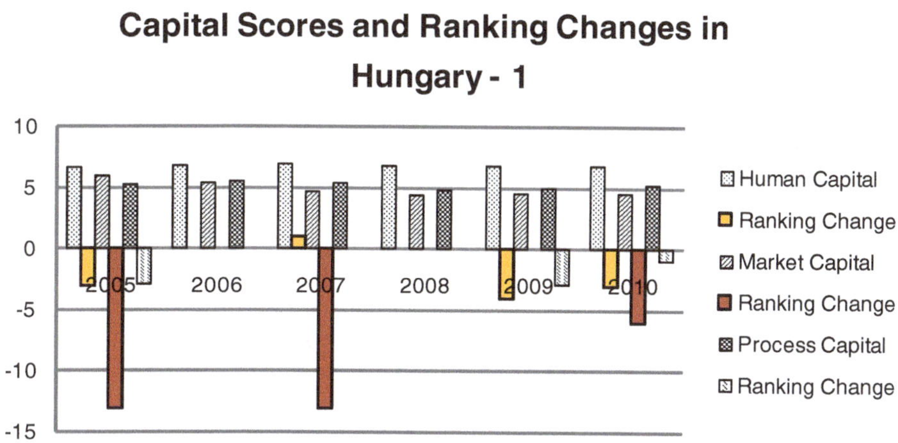

Fig. 3.21 Human capital, market capital, process capital, and ranking changes in Hungary

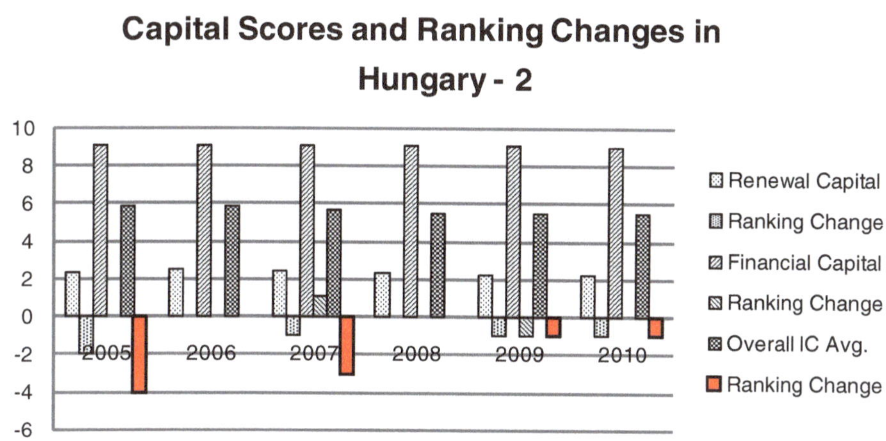

Fig. 3.22 Renewal capital, financial capital, average NIC, and ranking changes in Hungary

Czech Republic. The last two negative numbers in its human capital and market capital indicate that the country lost some international competitiveness in these two capitals, comparing the most recent period (2009–2010) with 2007–2008 and 6-year average.

Figure 3.20 and Table 3.2 show that the Czech Republic had minor ranking changes in terms of renewal capital, financial capital, and average NIC, ranging from −1 to +1.

From Fig. 3.21 and Table 3.2, Hungary's human capital ranking changes (−3, 1, −4, −3) indicate that the country was losing international competitiveness in human capital. The large scale ranking lost (−13, −13, 0, −6) for market capital indicates that Hungary was drastically losing international competitiveness in

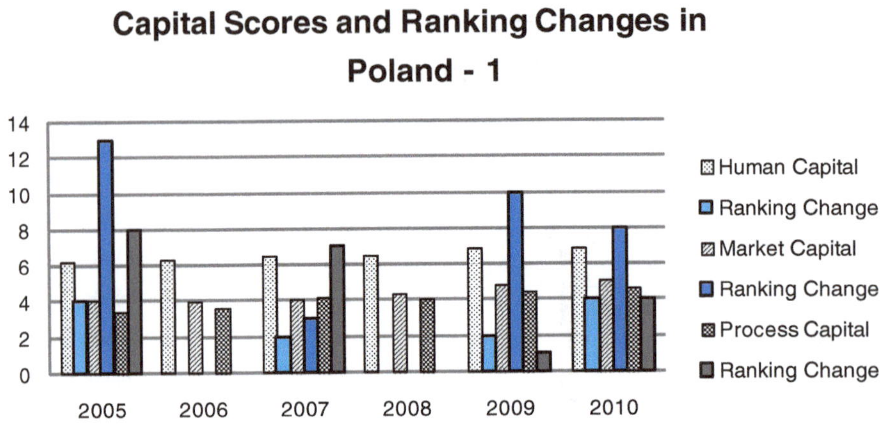

Fig. 3.23 Human capital, market capital, process capital, and ranking changes in Poland

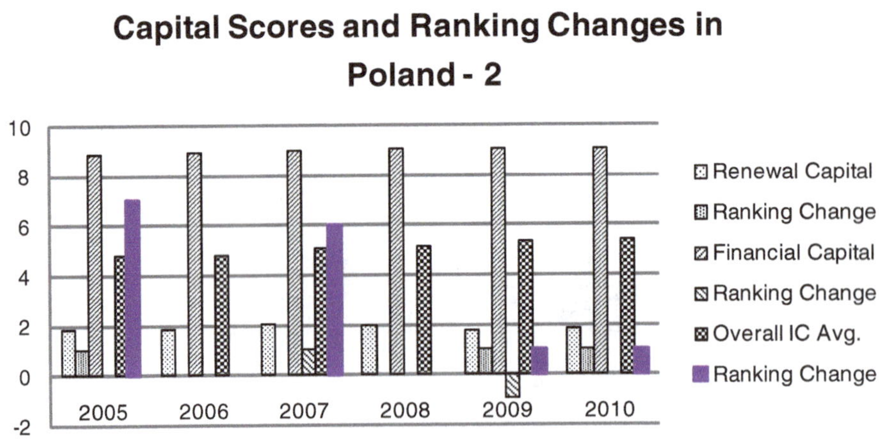

Fig. 3.24 Renewal capital, financial capital, average NIC, and ranking changes in Poland

market capital after the financial crisis. The ranking changes (−3, 0, −3, −1) of process capital also shows that Hungary decreased its international competitiveness in process capital, however with a relatively smaller scale.

Figure 3.22 and Table 3.2 show that the ranking changes of renewal capital (−2, −1, −1, −1) and financial capital (0, 1, −1, 0) were less than that of its average NIC (−4, −3, −1, −1). In general, most of the ranking comparisons are negative in Hungary, except two small ranking gains only (human capital and financial capital). Particularly, it has the largest scale of ranking drop (−13) in market capital. Such finding indicates that Hungary was losing its intangible assets competitiveness after the financial crisis.

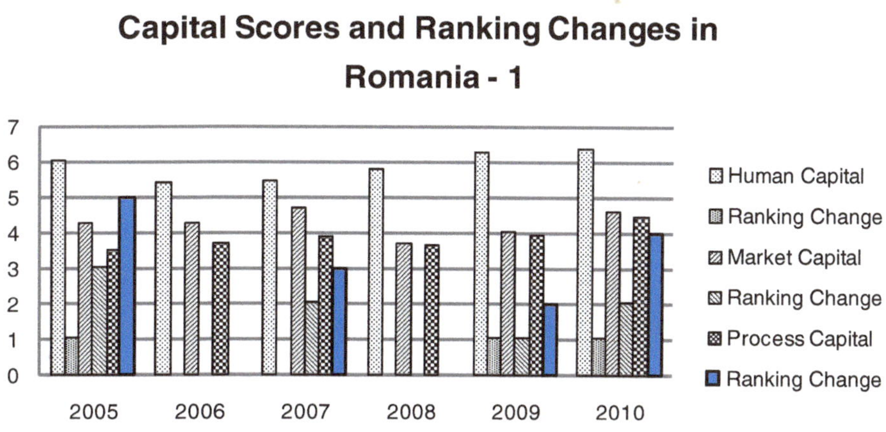

Fig. 3.25 Human capital, market capital, process capital, and ranking changes in Romania

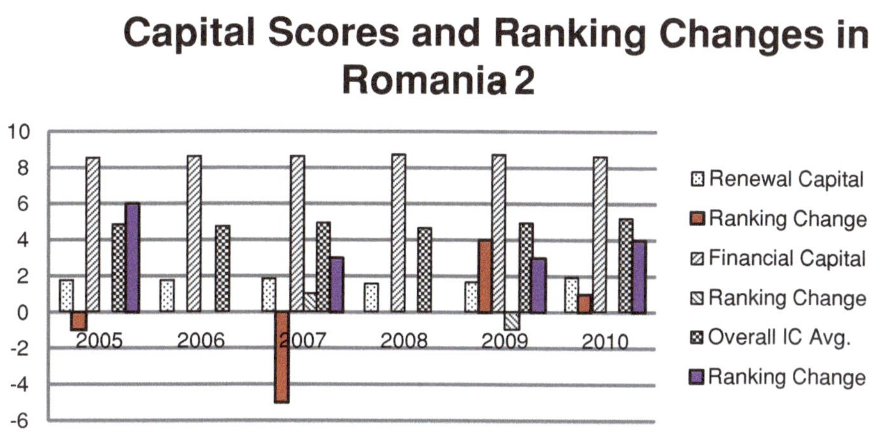

Fig. 3.26 Renewal capital, financial capital, average NIC, and ranking changes in Romania

From Fig. 3.23 and Table 3.2, Poland's human capital ranking changes (4, 2, 2, 4) indicate that the country was gaining international competitiveness in human capital. Its large scale ranking gains (13, 3, 10, 8) for market capital is eye-opening and explains well the country's outstanding performance during and after the financial crisis. Similar positive ranking changes (8, 7, 1, 4) of Poland's process capital has the same connotation with that of its market capital, only having a smaller scale.

Figure 3.24 and Table 3.2 show that the ranking changes of renewal capital (1, 0, 1, 1), financial capital (0, 1, −1, 0), and average NIC (7, 6, 1, 1) indicate that Poland has relatively mild ranking progress in renewal capital and financial capital. Yet, it also gained in NIC international competitiveness after the financial

Table 3.2 Ranking changes in three time periods for Bulgaria, the Czech Republic, Hungary, Poland, and Romania

	(1st period–3rd period)	1st period 2005–2006	2nd period 2007–2008		3rd period 2009–2010		2005–2010 average NIC48 ranking	
	Difference#1	Ranking	Ranking	Difference	Ranking	Difference	NIC 48 ranking	Difference
Human capital								
Bulgaria	**−3**	34	31	**3**	37	**−6**	34	**−3**
Czech Republic	**−1**	31	29	**2**	32	**−3**	30	**−2**
Hungary	**−3**	24	23	**1**	27	**−4**	24	**−3**
Poland	**4**	29	27	**2**	25	**2**	29	**4**
Romania	**1**	32	32	**0**	31	**1**	32	**1**
Market Capital								
Bulgaria	**6**	36	27	**9**	30	**−3**	31	**1**
Czech Republic	**0**	20	16	**4**	20	**−4**	18	**−2**
Hungary	**−13**	25	38	**−13**	38	**0**	32	**−6**
Poland	**13**	46	43	**3**	33	**10**	41	**8**
Romania	**3**	43	41	**2**	40	**1**	42	**2**
Process Capital								
Bulgaria	**2**	38	33	**5**	36	**−3**	36	**0**
Czech Republic	**−1**	23	26	**−3**	24	**2**	25	**1**
Hungary	**−3**	27	27	**0**	30	**−3**	29	**−1**
Poland	**8**	42	35	**7**	34	**1**	38	**4**
Romania	**5**	40	37	**3**	35	**2**	39	**4**
Renewal Capital								
Bulgaria	**−3**	38	42	**−4**	41	**1**	41	**0**
Czech Republic	**0**	24	23	**1**	24	**−1**	24	**0**
Hungary	**−2**	28	29	**−1**	30	**−1**	29	**−1**
Poland	**1**	35	35	**0**	34	**1**	35	**1**
Romania	**−1**	36	41	**−5**	37	**4**	38	**1**
Financial Capital								

(continued)

Table 3.2 (continued)

	(1st period–3rd period)	1st period 2005–2006	2nd period 2007–2008		3rd period 2009–2010		2005–2010 average NIC48 ranking	
	Difference#1	Ranking	Ranking	Difference	Ranking	Difference	NIC 48 ranking	Difference
Bulgaria	**1**	38	36	**2**	37	**−1**	37	**0**
Czech Republic	**0**	27	26	**1**	27	**−1**	27	**0**
Hungary	**0**	29	28	**1**	29	**−1**	29	**0**
Poland	**0**	30	29	**1**	30	**−1**	30	**0**
Romania	**0**	39	38	**1**	39	**−1**	39	**0**
NIC								
Bulgaria	**−2**	35	33	**2**	37	**−4**	35	**−2**
Czech Republic	**0**	25	24	**1**	25	**−1**	25	**0**
Hungary	**−4**	26	29	**−3**	30	**−1**	29	**−1**
Poland	**7**	38	32	**6**	31	**1**	32	**1**
Romania	**6**	41	38	**3**	35	**3**	39	**4**

#Remarks

1. The second column compares the 3rd (2009–2010) period ranking with the 1st (2005–2006)
2. The fifth column compares the 2nd (2007–2008) period ranking with the 1st (2005–2006)
3. The seventh column compares the 3rd (2009–2010) period ranking with the 2nd (2007–2008)
4. The last column compares the most current 3rd period ranking (2009–2010) with the original six-year average NIC48 ranking summarized in Table 3.1

crisis. In general, the ranking changes of Poland are the opposite of Hungary's, the former with relatively large scale ranking gains and the latter with relatively large scale ranking losses.

From Fig. 3.25 and Table 3.2, Romania's human capital ranking changes (1, 0, 1, 1) are minor. The ranking gains (3, 2, 1, 2) for market capital and (5, 3, 2, 4) for process capital indicate that Romania was improving international competitiveness in both capitals during and after the financial crisis.

Figure 3.26 and Table 3.2 show that the ranking changes of renewal capital (−1, −5, 4, 1), financial capital (0, 1, −1, 0), and average NIC (6, 3, 3, 4) indicate that Romania temporarily lost its renewal capital international competitiveness during the financial crisis; yet regained the ranking after the crisis. Romania especially improves its NIC international competitiveness after the financial crisis with its all positive and relatively large scale NIC ranking gains. In general, Romania had good ranking progress in market capital, process capital and NIC after the financial crisis.

In summary, within this country cluster, human capital for Bulgaria, the Czech Republic, and Hungary lost international competitiveness after the financial crisis; whereas Poland experienced ranking gains. For market capital, Poland had relatively large scale and Romania had smaller scale ranking gain; whereas Hungary had the largest scale ranking drops. For process capital, Poland had relatively large scale and Romania had smaller scale ranking gains; whereas Hungary had small scale ranking drops. For renewal capital, Bulgaria and Romania had temporary ranking drops during the financial crisis, yet regained the ranking after the financial crisis. Ranking changes of 1–10 scaled financial capital are minor for all countries. For average NIC, Poland and Romania were gaining their international competitiveness in a relatively large scale, whereas Bulgaria and Hungary were losing their international competitiveness after the financial crisis. By eyeballing Figs. 3.17, 3.18, 3.19, 3.20, 3.21, 3.22, 3.23, 3.24, 3.25, 3.26, Hungary had the largest number of ranking declines and Poland had the most impressive ranking gains.

An important finding of this section is that internal improvement does not guarantee external international competitiveness. An example is Bulgaria's human capital. Over the six years, its score decreased a minute 0.03 point (5.54–5.51 in Fig. 3.1), yet it experienced a relatively large scale ranking drop of 3 and six ranks. Therefore, a country's internal score change needs to be examined together with external competitiveness to get a fuller picture of its relative position in the international arena.

3-Dimensional National Intellectual Capital Trajectory

Up to this section, all the figures plotted different combinations of various capitals, capital-GDP co-development, and ranking changes on a flat plane. Even though Figs. 3.7, 3.8, 3.9, 3.10, 3.11, 3.12 displayed four dimensions with color and bubble size as the 3rd and 4th dimension in addition to x axis and y axis, graphically they are still on one plane. This section presents three-dimensional (3D) graphs showing each country's NIC development trajectory on a 48-country 3D landscape of various types. Since NIC evolution over time is always complex, combining different views from different angles may provide more comprehensive perspectives.

In what follows, we first explore the value driving context by uncovering influencing factors of GDP growth for Bulgaria, the Czech Republic, Hungary, Poland, and Romania from 2005 to 2010. Second, in explaining the GDP growth, we present the high, middle and low capability which human capital, market capital, process capital, and renewal capital respectively have. Third, we examine the efficiency (GDP growth) enhancing factors and impeding factors of each country, taking each country's turning point into consideration. Last, we identify the efficiency drivers of each country in reaching a targeted GDP.

Figure 3.27 shows a rectangular 3D landscape, with a longer north–south side. The formation of the landscape is based on the data of 29 national intellectual capital indicators (presented in Appendix 3) for 48 countries covering six years (2005–2010), with a total of 8,352 (29 × 48 × 6) data points. In other words, Fig. 3.27 is the aggregated NIC landscape of the 48 countries. The relative NIC positions of Bulgaria, the Czech Republic, Hungary, Poland, and Romania (pointed out with arrows) are in the middle left side and lower part of the landscape. The enlarged trails indicate the NIC progression (upward), regression (downward), or changing configuration (sideward) of each country over the six years. Each white trail on the landscape represents a country. The altitude coloring from purple (north), dark blue, blue, green, yellow, and red (south) is computer generated, according to GDP values, with purple representing high GDP descending to low GDP in red.

Figures 3.28, 3.29, and 3.30 are a set. Figure 3.28 presents four graphs indicating the high capability region of each human capital, market capital, process capital, and renewal capital in explaining the GDP growth. High capability means the data points are 20 % above the mean value of each capital. This figure shows that none of the human capital, market capital, process capital, and renewal capital of these five emerging European countries is in the high capability region.

Figure 3.29 displays another four graphs indicating the middle capability region of each human capital, market capital, process capital, and renewal capital in explaining the GDP growth. Middle capability means the data points are within the top 50 % value of each capital. This figure shows that the human capitals of Hungary and Poland are in the middle capability region. In addition, the market capital and process capital of the Czech Republic are also in the middle capability region.

Figure 3.30 shows the last four graphs in this set indicating the low capability region of each human capital, market capital, process capital, and renewal capital in explaining the GDP growth. Low capability means the data points are 20 % below the mean value of each capital. This figure shows that most of the capitals of these five countries (except as described in Fig. 3.29) are in the low capability region.

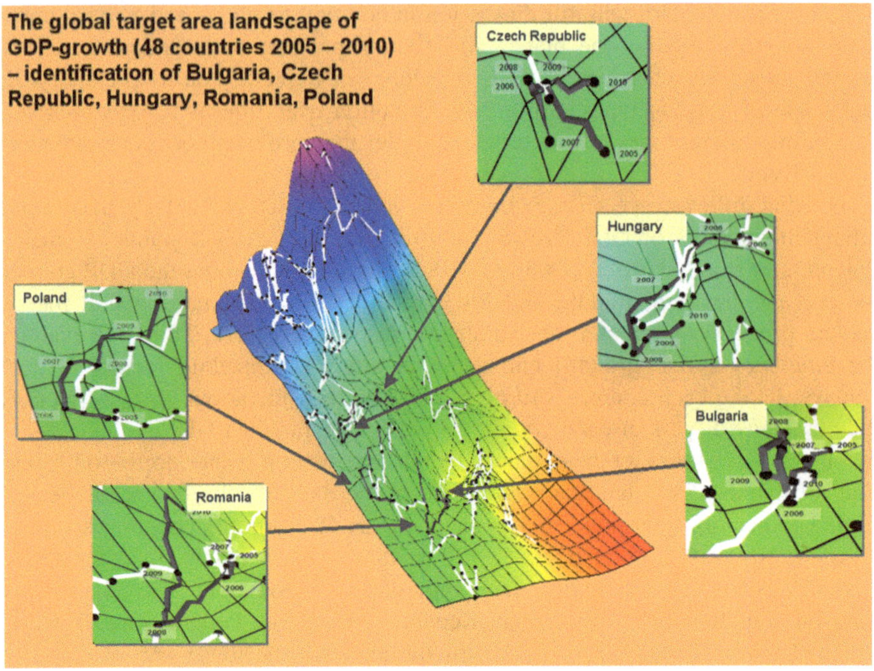

Fig. 3.27 The NIC trail of Bulgaria, the Czech Republic, Hungary, Poland, and Romania on a 3D 48-country landscape

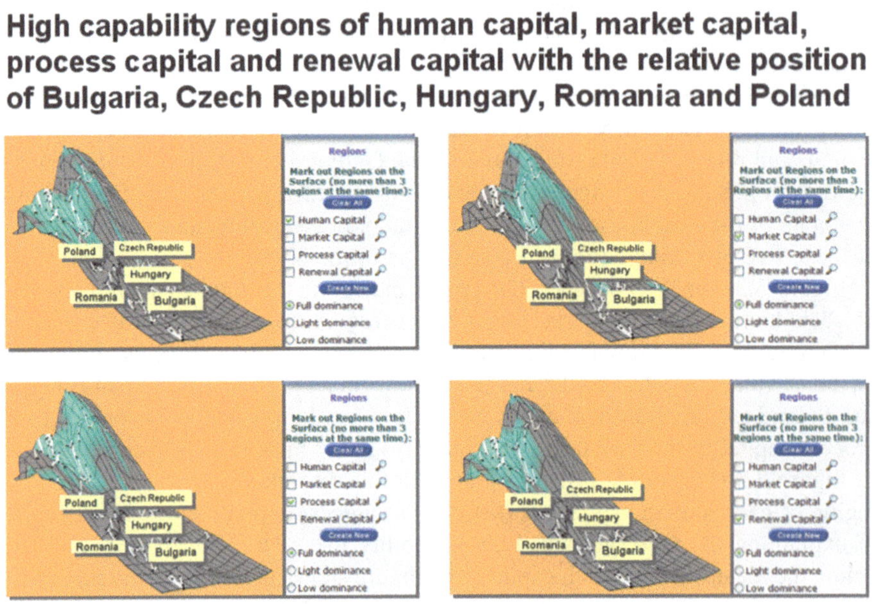

Fig. 3.28 The high capability region of human capital, market capital, process capital, and renewal capital

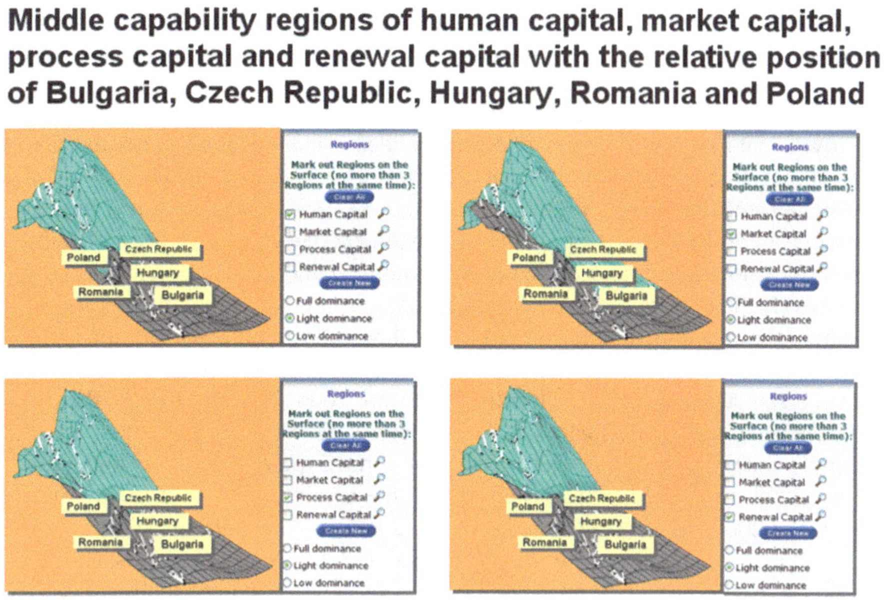

Fig. 3.29 The middle capability region of human capital, market capital, process capital, and renewal capital

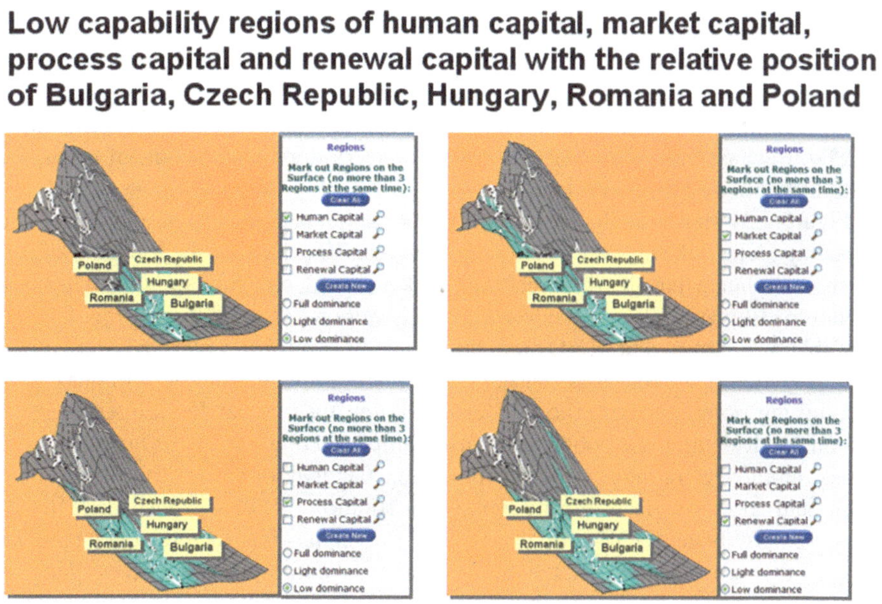

Fig. 3.30 The low capability region of human capital, market capital, process capital, and renewal capital

In general, the three figures as a set explain that NIC of these five countries are generally 20 % below average in explaining GDP growth. Even though the Czech Republic is classified by the World Economic Forum as Stage 3 innovation driven developed country, its long-term NIC human capital and renewal capital are still in the low capability region. This finding provides a clear guidance for the Czech Republic to plan its next level of national development.

Another set of figures, Figs. 3.31, 3.32, 3.33, 3.34, 3.35 display efficiency-enhancing or efficiency-impeding factors that affect GDP growth before and after the NIC turning point for Bulgaria, the Czech Republic, Hungary, Poland, and Romania, respectively. The white indicator boxes at the upper right display the results of the enhancing or impeding factors. We employed three or four rounds of data analysis for each country, depending on whether the country has one or multiple NIC turning points. For instance, Bulgaria's turning points are 2006, 2008, and 2009; therefore, we traced the explaining factors of 2005 against 2006 (starting point → the first turning point), 2006 against 2008 (the first turning point → the second turning point), 2008 against 2009 (one year before the turning point → the last turning point), and 2009 against 2010 (the last turning point → the ending point).

As an easy reference, we summarize in Table 3.3 two sets of results, each with the first five key factors. If there is a clear score cutting point (such as less than 1 % in the white indicator boxes), the reported factors may be less than five. The first set displays the efficiency enhancing and impeding factors before the turning point, the second set exhibits the efficiency enhancing and impeding indicators after the (last) turning point in italic letters. Since the factor strength (percentage) varies with different explaining power, we have calculated the average weight of the five enhancing and impeding factors and display each respective percentage in the rows for "Factor #5". We also count the frequency of four more frequently displayed categories, namely government related issues (G), human capital related issues (H), market capital related issues (M), and research and development issues (R&D). Because capital availability was a concern during the financial crisis, we particularly highlighted this factor as "G-C."

Figure 3.31 shows the turning points (2006, 2008, and 2009), the enhancing and impeding factors of Bulgaria. The four rectangular 3D graphs on the left hand side of the figure indicate that all human capital, market capital, process capital, and renewal capital for Bulgaria fall into the low capability region (20 % below average).

Table 3.3 shows that R&D and human capital related issues are the major impeding factors for Bulgaria. Basic research is an impeding factor both before the first turning point and after the last turning point. Insufficient IP rights protection and university-enterprise cooperation also hamper GDP growth. For human capital issues, employee training is the 5th impeding factor both before the first turning point and after the last turning point. In addition, skilled labor needs to be improved for better GDP growth as well. For enhancing factors, data analysis reveals that government related issues, such as corporate tax encouragement, government efficiency, fair business competition environment, and capital availability facilitate Bulgaria's GDP growth.

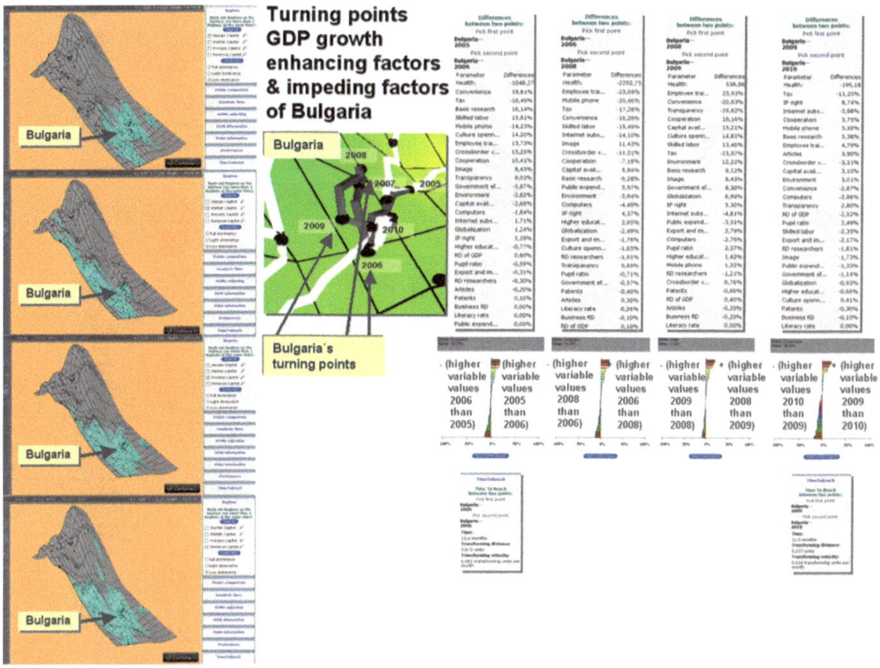

Fig. 3.31 Turning point and GDP growth enhancing and impeding factors of Bulgaria

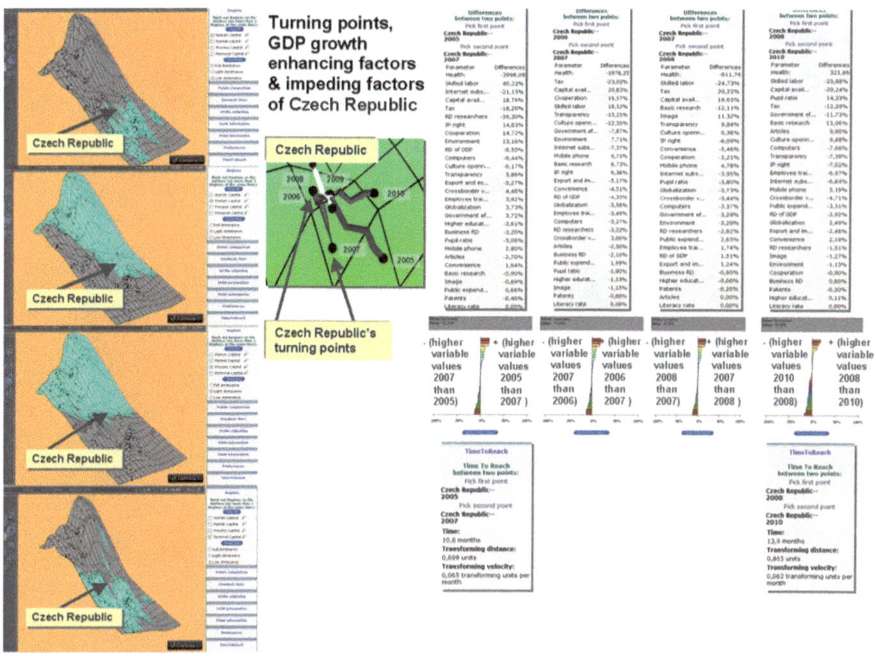

Fig. 3.32 Turning point and GDP growth enhancing and impeding factors of the Czech Republic

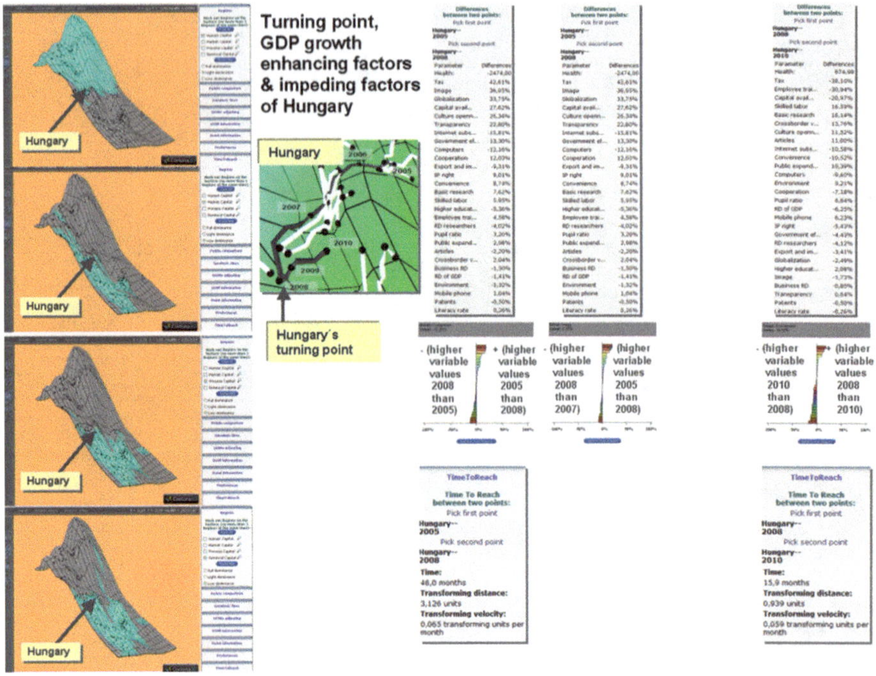

Fig. 3.33 Turning point and GDP growth enhancing and impeding factors of Hungary

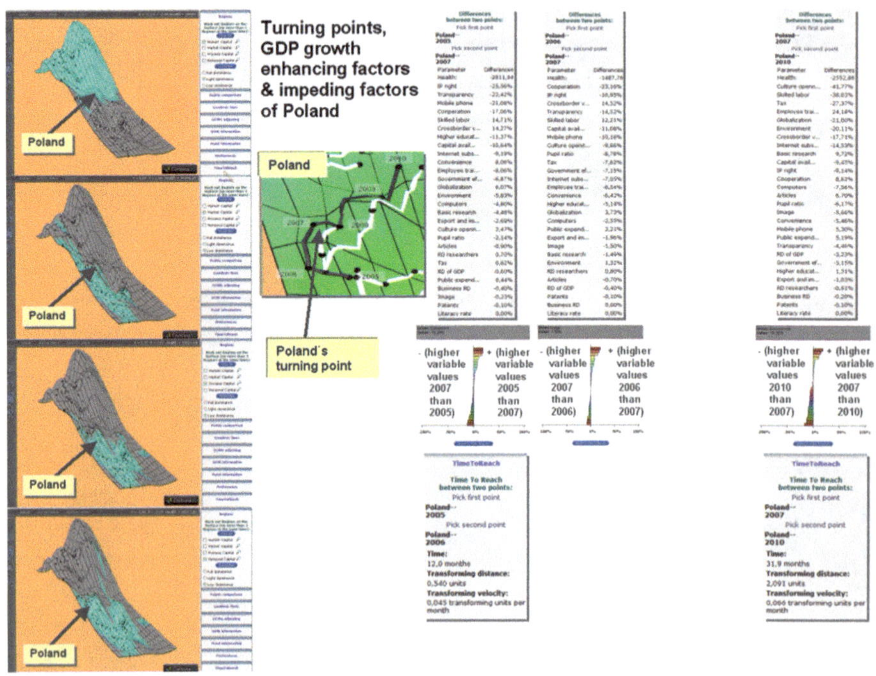

Fig. 3.34 Turning point and GDP growth enhancing and impeding factors of Poland

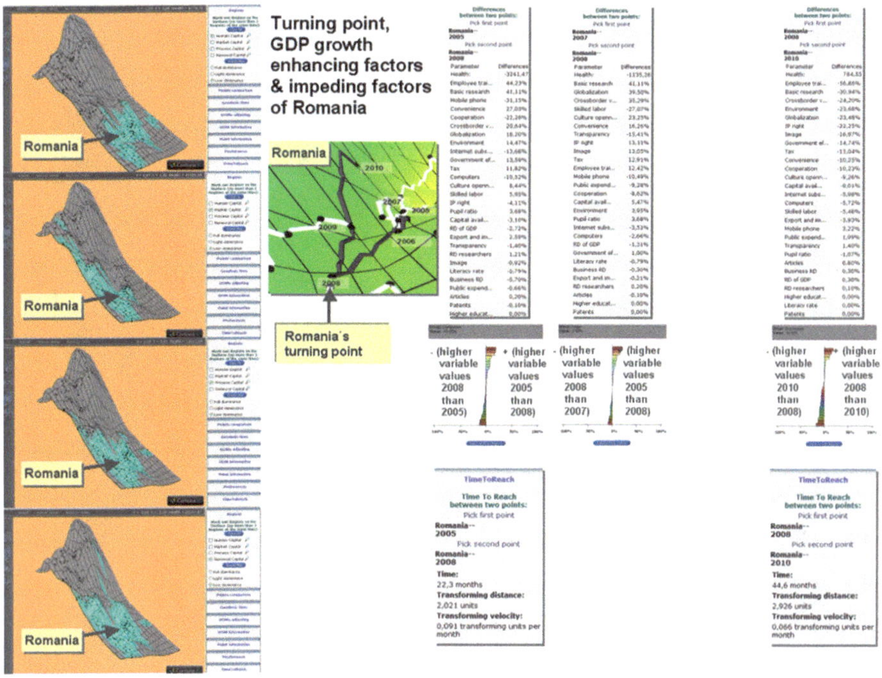

Fig. 3.35 Turning point and GDP growth enhancing and impeding factors of Romania

Figure 3.32 shows the turning points (2006 and 2008), the enhancing and impeding factors of the Czech Republic. The four rectangular 3D graphs on the left hand side of the figure indicate that human capital and renewal capital for the Czech Republic fall into the low capability region (20 % below average), whereas its market capital and process capital are in the middle capability region (top 50 %).

Table 3.3 shows that R&D related issues constitute the major impeding factors for the Czech Republic, including basic research, IP rights protection, scientific articles, and university-enterprise cooperation. Government related impeding factors include capital availability and fair business competition environment. In addition, skilled labor and pupil-teacher ratio also need improvement. There are two good signs; two impeding factors—skilled labor and capital availability—before the first turning point were turned into enhancing factors after the last turning point. For enhancing factors, data analysis reveals that government related issues, including corporate tax encouragement, capital availability, and government efficiency facilitate the Czech Republic's GDP growth.

Figure 3.33 shows the 2008 turning point, the enhancing and impeding factors of Hungary. The four rectangular 3D graphs on the left hand side of the figure indicate that human capital is in the middle capability region (top 50 %), whereas market capital, process capital, and renewal capital for Hungary fall into the low capability region (20 % below average).

Table 3.3 Enhancing factors and impeding factors of GDP per capita (ppp) growth for the five emerging European countries −2/2

Influencing factor	Bulgaria Enhancing factors	Bulgaria Impeding factors	Czech Republic Enhancing factors	Czech Republic Impeding factors	Hungary Enhancing factors	Hungary Impeding factors
Factor #1 before (1st) turning point	Corporate tax encouragement (G)	Convenience of establishing new firms (G)	Internet subscribers	Skilled labor (H)	Internet subscribers	Corporate tax encouragement (G)
Factor#1 after (last) turning point	*Corporate tax encouragement* (G)	*IP rights protection* (R&D)	*Skilled labor* (H)	*Pupil-teacher ratio* (H)	*Corporate tax encouragement* (G)	*Skilled labor* (H)
Factor #2 before (1st) turning point	Mobile phone subscribers	Basic research (R&D)	Corporate tax encouragement (G)	Capital availability (G-C)	Computers in use per capita	Image of country (M)
Factor #2 after (last) turning point	*Internet subscribers*	*University-enterprise cooperation* (R&D)	*Capital availability* (G-C)	*Basic research* (R&D)	*Employee training* (H)	*Basic research* (R&D)
Factor #3 before (1st) turning point	Government efficiency (G)	Skilled labor (H)	R&D researchers (R&D)	IP rights protection (R&D)	Export of goods (M)	Globalization (M)
Factor #3 after (last) turning point	*Cross-border ventures* (M)	*Mobile phone subscribers*	*Corporate tax encouragement* (G)	*Scientific articles* (R&D)	*Capital availability* (G-C)	*Cross-border ventures* (M)
Factor #4 before (1st) turning point	Fair business competition environment (G)	Openness of culture (M)	R&D % GDP (R&D)	University-enterprise cooperation (R&D)	Higher education enrollment (H)	Capital availability (G-C)
Factor #4 after (last) turning point	*Convenience of establishing new firms* (G)	*Basic research* (R&D)	*Government efficiency* (G)	*Openness of culture* (M)	*Internet subscribers*	*Openness of culture* (M)
Factor #5 before (1st) turning point	Capital availability (G-C)	Employee training (H)	Computers in use per capita	Fair business competition environment (G)	R&D researchers (R&D)	Openness of culture (M)
	(Average weight—8.41 %) #	**(Average weight—5.94 %)#**	**(Average weight—13.73 %)**	**(Average weight—20.34 %)**	**(Average weight—9.33 %)**	**(Average weight—33.45 %)**
Factor #5 after (last) turning point	*Computers in use per capita*	*Employee training* (H)	*Computers in use per capita*	*Mobile phone subscribers*	*Convenience of establishing new firms* (G)	*Scientific articles* (R&D)
	(Average weight—5.27 %)	**(Average weight—6.03 %)**	**(Average weight—15.58 %)**	**(Average weight—10.05 %)**	**(Average weight—22.22 %)**	**(Average weight—13.80 %)**
Category frequency count	G-6 H-0 M-1 R&D-0	G-1 H-3 M-1 R&D-4	G-4 H-1 M-0 R&D-2	G-2 H-2 M-1 R&D-4	G-3 H-2 M-1 R&D-1	G-2 H-1 M-5 R&D-2

(continued)

Table 3.3 (continued)

Influencing factor	Poland Enhancing factors	Poland Impeding factors	Romania Enhancing factors	Romania Impeding factors
Factor #1 before (1st) turning point	IP rights protection (R&D)	Skilled labor (H)	Mobile phone subscribers	Employee training (H)
Factor#1 after (last) turning point	*Openness of culture* (M)	*Employee training* (H)	*Employee training* (H)	*Mobile phone subscribers*
Factor #2 before (1st) turning point	Transparency of government policy (G)	Cross-border ventures (M)	University-enterprise cooperation (R&D)	Basic research (R&D)
Factor #2 after (last) turning point	*Skilled labor* (H)	*Basic research* (R&D)	*Basic research* (R&D)	*Public expenditure on education* (H)
Factor #3 before (1st) turning point	Mobile phone subscribers	Convenience of establishing new firms (G)	Internet subscribers	Convenience of establishing new firms (G)
Factor #3 after (last) turning point	*Corporate tax encouragement* (G)	*University-enterprise cooperation* (R&D)	*Cross-border ventures* (M)	*Transparency of government policy* (G)
Factor #4 before (1st) turning point	University-enterprise cooperation (R&D)	Globalization (M)	Computers in use per capita	Cross-border ventures (M)
Factor #4 after (last) turning point	*Globalization* (M)	*Scientific articles* (R&D)	*Fair business competition environment* (G)	–
Factor #5 before (1st) turning point	Higher education enrollment (H) **(Average weight—19.50 %)**	Openness of culture (M) **(Average weight—9.12 %)**	IP rights protection (R&D) **(Average weight—-16.34 %)**	Globalization (M) **(Average weight—30.25 %)**
Factor #5 after (last) turning point	*Fair business competition environment* (G) **(Average weight-29.66 %)**	*Mobile phone subscribers* **(Average weight-10.90 %)**	*Globalization* (M) **(Average weight-31.83 %)**	– **(Average weight-2.20 %)**
Category frequency count	G-3 H-2 M-2 R&D-2	G-1 H-2 M-3 R&D-3	G-1 H-1 M-2 R&D-3	G-2 H-2 M-2 R&D-1
Category frequency count—Grand total	G-17 H-6 M-6 R&D-8	G-8 H-10 M-12 R&D-14		

Remarks: (G & G-C)—government related issues including capital availability represented by G-C (total 25 counts including 4 counts of capital availability), (H)—human capital issues (16 counts), (M)—market capital issues (18 counts), (R&D)—research and development (22 counts)
#: average weight of each enhancing/impeding factor before and after the turning point

Table 3.3 shows that market capital related issues constitute the major impeding factors for Hungary, including image of country, globalization, cross-border ventures, and openness of culture. Openness of culture is an impeding factor for both before and after the turning point. Two governments related impeding factors—corporate tax encouragement and capital availability before the turning point were turned into enhancing factors after the turning point. Two R&D impeding factors—basic research and scientific articles need improvement. For enhancing factors, data analysis reveals that government related issues, including corporate tax encouragement, capital availability, and convenience of establishing new firms facilitate Hungary's GDP growth.

Figure 3.34 shows the 2007 turning point, the enhancing and impeding factors of Poland. The four rectangular 3D graphs on the left hand side of the figure indicate that human capital is in the middle capability region (top 50 %), whereas market capital, process capital, and renewal capital for Poland fall into the low capability region (20 % below average).

Table 3.3 shows that market capital and R&D related issues constitute the major impeding factors for Poland. Insufficient cross-border ventures, globalization, and openness of culture hamper Poland's GDP growth. However, globalization and openness of culture before the turning point have been turned into enhancing factors after the turning point. R&D related impeding factors include basic research, university-enterprise cooperation, and scientific articles. For enhancing factors, data analysis reveals that government related issues, including transparency of government policy, corporate tax encouragement, and fair business competition environment facilitate Poland's GDP growth.

Figure 3.35 shows the 2008 turning point, the enhancing and impeding factors of Romania. The four rectangular 3D graphs on the left hand side of the figure indicate that all human capital, market capital, process capital and renewal capital for Romania fall into the low capability region (20 % below average).

Table 3.3 shows that government, human capital, and market capital related issues count two each of the major impeding factors for Romania. Convenience of establishing new firms and transparency of government policy need improvement for a better GDP growth. Employee training and public expenditure on education have to be strengthened. In addition, cross-border ventures and globalization are insufficient. However, employee training, cross-border ventures, and globalization before the turning point have been turned into enhancing factors after the turning point. For enhancing factors, data analysis reveals that R&D related issues, including university-enterprise cooperation, basic research, and IP rights protection facilitate Romania's GDP growth.

For impeding factors, the average weight before the turning point is higher than after the turning point in Bulgaria (15.94 vs. 6.03 %), the Czech Republic (20.34 vs. 10.05 %), Hungary (33.45 vs. 13.80 %), and Romania (30.25 vs. 2.20 %). This result reflects that the impeding factors for these countries were less stressful after the financial crisis. Only Poland has a slightly higher weight after than before the turning point (10.90 vs. 9.12 %). For enhancing factors, except Bulgaria, the average weight after the turning point is higher than before the turning point.

To summarize Table 3.3 into an overall suggestion, we count the frequency of both enhancing and impeding factors by categories for all the five countries, shown in the last row of the table. There are a total of 25 counts of government-related issues (G & G-C), including 4 counts of capital availability (G-C). Among which there are 8 counts of impeding factors, including convenience of establishing new firms, capital availability, fair business competition environment, and corporate tax encouragement. The Czech Republic, Hungary, and Romania have two counts each of government related issues as the impeding factors.

There are 16 counts of human capital issues (H). Among which there are 10 counts of impeding factors, including skilled labor, employee training, pupil-teacher ratio, and public expenditure on education. There are 18 counts of market capital issues (M). Among these, 12 counts are impeding factors, including openness of culture, image of country, cross-border ventures, and globalization. For research and development issues (R&D) there are 22 counts, among which impeding factors total 14 counts, including IP rights protection, basic research, university-enterprise cooperation, and scientific articles.

Figure 3.36 identifies the efficiency drivers (positive term) for each individual country. Efficiency targeting is akin to benchmarking. Efficiency represents GDP in this 3D software program. Since Germany stands out to be the most resilient country in the 2008 European Union financial turmoil, therefore it serves as a good benchmarking target for these five emerging European countries. In Fig. 3.36, the stacked small horizontal stripes are the deficiency factors of each country benchmarked against the GDP of Germany in 2010. The length of the stripes represents the degree of deficiency. For easier comparison, we list the first five deficiency factors of each country in Table 3.4.

The results indicate that Bulgaria needs to strengthen, in sequence, its university-enterprise cooperation, employee training, IP rights protection, fair business competition environment, and basic research. The Czech Republic needs to strengthen its patents, university-enterprise cooperation, basic research, business R&D, and fair business competition environment. Hungary needs to strengthen its basic research, patents, image of country, business R&D, and transparency of government policy. Poland needs to strengthen its employee training, basic research, patents, business R&D, and university-enterprise cooperation. Romania needs to strengthen its computers in use per capita, patents, R&D % of GDP, business R&D, and R&D researchers.

With Germany being used as a benchmarking country, irrespective to the sequence of deficiency, the common areas (in frequency count) that these five countries need to improve include basic research (4 counts), business R&D (4 counts), patents (4 counts), university-enterprise cooperation (3 counts), fair business competition environment (2 counts), and employee training (2 counts). That is, the areas that need improvement are quite similar for these five countries. Among the above six common indicators, four (basic research, business R&D, patents, and university-enterprise cooperation) are R&D related issues. In other words, to reach the level similar to Germany's economic development, these five emerging European countries need to greatly enhance their R&D capability. Based

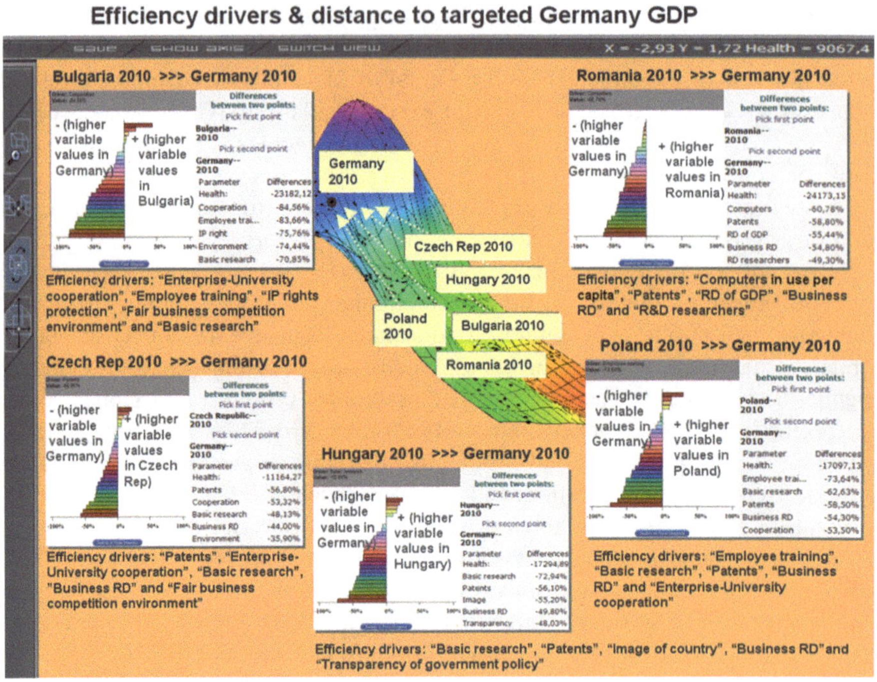

Fig. 3.36 Efficiency drivers and distance to targeted GDP of Germany

on the average deficiency (negative term) percentage reported in Table 3.4 and Fig. 3.36, Bulgaria (−77.85 %) has the most amount of work to do in order to achieve the target GDP, followed by Poland (−60.51 %), Hungary (−56.41 %), Roman (−55.82 %) and the Czech Republic (−47.63 %). In other words, the Czech Republic will have the shortest route to reach the preset GDP goal through enhancing its R&D capability, such as university-enterprise cooperation and business R&D.

The added value of the above 3D trajectory analysis is to (1) display the NIC trails of the discussed countries on a 48-country landscape; (2) locate the capability region of the four individual capitals for each country; (3) highlight NIC turning points, details of the enhancing or impeding factors, and the dynamics of factor changes for each country; and (4) calculate the distance that each country has to progress in order to achieve the benchmark GDP and identify the first five key factors to reach this goal. This section supplements the previous sections by looking into the contribution of each individual indicator in each year, rather than average scores and average rankings.

In this chapter, we reported our research findings in layman terms with graphs and tables of various types for easier reading. This study on national intangible assets has uncovered some important findings that are not apparent in other GDP related studies. For instance, the contribution of renewal capital to GDP growth is

Table 3.4 The first five efficiency drivers targeting GDP of Germany

Efficiency driver	Bulgaria	Czech Republic	Hungary	Poland	Romania
Factor #1	University-enterprise cooperation	Patents	Basic research	Employee training	Computers in use per capita
Factor #2	Employee training	University-enterprise cooperation	Patents	Basic research	Patents
Factor #3	IP rights protection	Basic research	Image of country	Patents	R&D % GDP
Factor #4	Fair business competition environment	Business R&D	Business R&D	Business R&D	Business R&D
Factor #5	Basic research	Fair business competition environment	Transparency of government policy	University- enterprise cooperation	R&D researchers
Average deficiency percentage of the above 5 drivers	−77.85 %	−47.63 %	−56.41 %	−60.51 %	−55.82 %

more effective in less developed countries than in advanced countries; the distance to the target GDP for Romania (55.82 %) is shorter than that of Hungary (56.41 %) even though Romania is behind Hungary in most of economic and NIC indicators.

Chapter 4
Beyond the 2008 Global Financial Crisis

This chapter reports activities after 2010, a time commonly regarded as the aftermath of the 2008 global financial crisis (Kehoe 2010). Although sovereign debt problems still linger in the Euro zone as of late-2012, and Spain requested financial assistance in June 2012, we use 2010 as a cutoff point in order to be consistent with the reports of other country clusters in this booklet series. In what follows, we first introduce the general status of the European Union, information regarding multiple countries, and then the condition of each individual country.

Since early 2010, the Euro zone has been facing a major debt crisis. The governments of several countries in the zone accumulated what many consider to be unsustainable levels of government debt. The sovereign debt crisis developed as countries experienced higher deficits and growing debt, making governments increasingly unable to pay back the money they owed. As a result, several countries including Greece, Ireland, and Portugal had to turn to other European countries, European Central Bank (ECB), and the International Monetary Fund (IMF) for loans in order to avoid default.

With the unfolding of the debt crisis, the Central and Eastern European countries were seriously affected owing to the high integration of their financial sectors with the Euro countries. In May 2010, EU member states agreed upon the establishment of a US$633.6 billion (€440 billion) Euro zone Member State-guaranteed European Financial Stability Facility (EFSF), after bailing out Greece (Moloney 2010). The EFSF will provide loans to EU member states in financial trouble. If a country receives a loan from the EFSF, it will be subject to strict austerity measures such as tax and pension reform, decreases in public wages, and privatization of some industries. EU member states will guarantee the EFSF's bonds. Yet, the EFSF is scheduled to expire in 2013, at which time it will be replaced with a permanent crisis mechanism called the European Stabilization Mechanism (ESM). To avoid any future crises in the Euro zone, the ESM will provide loans to a member state that is threatened with severe economic difficulties and will require borrowers to follow austerity measures similar to those of the EFSF (Harrington 2011).

C. Y.-Y. Lin et al., *National Intellectual Capital and the Financial Crisis in Bulgaria, Czech Republic, Hungary, Romania, and Poland*, SpringerBriefs in Economics,
DOI: 10.1007/978-1-4614-8018-1_4,

The IMF extended financial aid to the five emerging European countries reported in this volume. In January 2010, the recovery of the industry sector in the reported region appeared as industrial production rose (Voinea et al. 2010). However, the upturn depends to a large extent on the revival of domestic demand and government facilitating policies as well. For building a more resilient economy after the financial crisis, the concept of smart growth, sustainable growth, and inclusive growth was promoted (Voinea et al. 2010). Smart growth relies on knowledge and innovation-based development, sustainable growth aims at building a more resource-efficient and greener economy, and inclusive growth strengthens the cohesion among economic, social, and territorial cohesion. In addition, EU also stressed the importance of economic coordination and surveillance across national borders to address countries' imbalances and divergences in real effective exchange rates (Voinea et al. 2010).

In what follows, we briefly describe what happened in each individual country after 2010.

Bulgaria

With the Bulgarian government's efforts in mitigating the negative impact of the financial crisis, the ratings agency Moody's upgraded its outlook on Bulgaria from stable to positive in January 2010 (QFinance 2012a). In the second quarter of 2010, signs of recovery appeared when a rebound in exports significantly reduced the pace of contraction in real GDP (CSD 2011). However, its GDP still stagnated with a 0.63 % real GDP growth in 2010, despite this significant recovery in exports (CIA 2012). Even though exports revived and current account deficit reduced from 8.5 % of GDP in 2009 to 5.5 % in 2010 (Social Watch 2010), the country's surplus turned into a −4 % of the GDP in 2010 (Minassian 2011). In the same year, unemployment increased from 6.8 % in 2009 to 10.2 % in 2010 (IMD data) with a great fall in the average permanent employment (Nonchev et al. 2011). During the third quarter of 2010, the share of employed people aged 15 and above out of the same-aged population was only 47.5 % and the number of employed people dropped by 175,800 compared to the same period in 2009 (Nonchev et al. 2011).

In 2010, Bulgarian government presented ambitious structural reform measures in the area of healthcare, education, the pension system, and public and revenue administration (European Union 2010). These measures aimed at enhancing the efficiency and effectiveness of public revenue and expenditure and increasing the growth potential of the economy to ensure sustainable convergence within the European Union (European Union 2010). Specifically, the government changed the costing and funding mechanism for health services and implemented stricter controls on healthcare spending (European Union 2010; QFinance 2012a). Reforms on tertiary education and R&D were also planned.

To curb the deteriorating deficit, the IMF recommended an urgent pensions system reform, including pensions freeze in 2010, smaller increases in pensions in the years ahead, and raising the retirement age or raising the minimum number of years of contributions to qualify for a pension (Social Watch 2010). As a result, the country's 2010 budget included a freeze in general pensions and public wages (QFinance 2012a). In terms of managing public state assets and public spending, optimization of existing structures, streamlining of public employment, and public administration were under way (European Union 2010). To facilitate the structural reforms and accelerate EU integration, Bulgarian government has identified the efficient use of the previously underutilized EU funds (only 20 % has been absorbed) as an important opportunity to finance public investments (World Bank 2012).

Going forward, the short-term to medium-term goal for Bulgaria is to secure a sustained process without compromising fiscal and macroeconomic stability (European Union 2010). The negative effects of demographic aging on potential output and the sustainability of public finances press the government to accelerate its pace of structural reforms with the aim of supporting potential growth.

In the wake of the global financial crisis, increased tensions in the markets are changing the external environment with significant downward adjustments to growth prospects (Ersado 2009). According to the April 2012 World Economic Outlook of the IMF, the Bulgarian economy is expected to grow by only 0.8 % in 2012 and will register a growth of 1.5 % in 2013 (Novinite 2012).

Czech Republic

Economy in the Czech Republic began to revive in 2010 and the country produced more than a million cars that year, over 80 % of which were exported (CIA 2012). To strengthen the economy, the Czech government implemented a fiscal consolidation and heavily weighted toward the revenue to make up the losses experienced in the wake of the crisis (OECD 2010a). As a result, fiscal consolidation reduced the general government deficit to 3.1 % of GDP in 2011, well below the government's target of 4.2 % of GDP (OECD 2012b). The Czech floating exchange rate remains the main shock absorber and its structural balance also improved by about one percentage point, reflecting reductions in the central government wage bill and better targeting of social assistance. The public debt to GDP ratio at 41.2 % at end 2011 remains manageable and attests to a strong fiscal position (IMF 2012c).

The Czech financial system has proved to be resilient to the effects of the global financial crisis. Czech banks do not depend on wholesale or external funding; instead, its banking sector is a net external creditor and the credit growth is funded mainly by domestic deposits (IMF 2012c). The Czech financial system remains profitable, reflecting a conservative structure of bank balance sheets and the low indebtedness of the corporate and household sectors (IMF 2012c). In 2010, Czech banks had the strongest loan-to-deposit ratio in the region of around 70 % (IMF 2012b; World Bank 2011).

Due to deteriorating external conditions, Czech post-crisis recovery stalled in 2011 (IMF 2012b). Since the Czech economy has no major internal imbalances, the major risks come from further unfavorable developments in the external environment (OECD 2012b). However, fiscal consolidation triggered a marked decline in government consumption, and the increase in the preferential VAT rate dampened consumer demand (OECD 2012b). Labor market conditions have deteriorated as the average real wage fell and unemployment increased since the second half of 2011 (OECD 2012b). GDP grew at a limited 1.5 % in 2011 (IMF 2012b). Following the slowdown in 2011, economic activity plummeted in the first quarter of 2012 affected by the Euro area weakness. In addition, the hike in the VAT rate and excise taxes, high oil prices and a weaker exchange rate are expected to temporarily increase inflation in 2012 (OECD 2012b).

Real GDP is projected to fall in 2012 owing to a decline in domestic consumption spurred by fiscal consolidation; however growth is expected in 2013 due to stronger exports and investments. OECD (2012a, 2012b) suggested the country to deepen its structural reforms to deregulate product markets for supporting investment growth and job creation. A potential intensification of the sovereign debt crisis in Europe would negatively affect the Czech economy through the trade channel. In addition, the Czech Republic's close financial integration with the Euro area makes such impact unavoidable. However, its strong fundamentals, including a manageable level of public debt, a comfortable external position, and a resilient financial system, limit the vulnerability against these risks (IMF 2012b).

After assessment, the IMF welcomed Czech government's plan to improve its fiscal framework, such as introducing a fiscal rule and an independent fiscal council. To curtail the costs and increase private participation, the continuation of pension, health, and tax reforms is important for securing long-term sustainability of the country. To improve international competitiveness, key priorities include developing infrastructure, improving labor market flexibility, and strengthening institutions and governance (IMF 2012c).

Hungary

The Hungarian economy rebounded in 2010 with a big boost from exports, especially to Germany. Real GDP growth turned positive to around 1.89 % (Fig. 2.1) in 2010. In 2010, there were some policy changes in the country including cutting business and personal income taxes, as well as imposed "crisis taxes" on financial institutions, energy, telecom companies, and retailers (CIA 2012). The country has also launched a special program of US$9.1 billion (HUF 1,800 billion, 6.5 % of GDP) to support the construction industry, hoping to start and complete 600 important investment projects to be spread over several years (Inotai 2010). Its stabilization program aimed at fiscal consolidation via government wage and pension bill reductions. In the banking sector, measures included a recapitalization of eligible banks and a strengthening of the supervisory and crisis management abilities (Dapontas 2011).

The government's austerity measures, imposed since late 2006, have reduced the budget deficit from over 9 % of its GDP in 2006 to 3.2 % in 2010 (CIA 2012). However, unemployment remained high, at more than 10 % in 2010. In 2011, Hungary's real GDP growth is 1.7 % based on Global Finance statistics (Global Finance 2012). In the same year, the country had a budget surplus, estimated to be between 2 % and 3 % of GDP, mainly due to higher one-off revenue stemming from the elimination of the obligatory private pension scheme (amounting to 9.75 % of GDP) (Hugh 2012). Despite the massive increase in exports since the end of the global financial crisis, the Hungarian GDP has recovered slowly. In addition, the global economic slowdown and heightened financial market stress have pushed Hungary's fragile and highly indebted economy back to recession at the end of 2011.

In the wake of the financial crisis, stabilizing the economy is the most pressing priority, strengthening the credibility and predictability of domestic policies is essential to developing an environment conducive to growth and confidence (OECD 2012c). However, since mid-2010, Hungary has implemented several policy measures that resulted in strongly-worded protests from the European Commission and the European Central Bank (EEAG 2012). In particular, the Hungarian government turned down a specific request from the European Commission in December 2011 to put on hold two pieces of legislation until further consultation (EEAG 2012). They were passed at the end of December 2011, including the National Bank of Hungary Act, which is viewed as a serious infringement of central bank independence. As a result, the IMF together with the European Commission was unwilling to step in with a new loan unless proper changes are made. However, the Hungarian government has made it clear that it has no intention of changing the proposed legislation. In 2012, the Hungarian government announced an increase in the VAT rate from 25 to 27 %, as well as increases in the social security contributions paid by firms and several other taxes (EEAG 2012).

According to EU advisory group, the Hungarian government's policies do not seem to address the main problems of the Hungarian economy, and may actually make them worse (EEAG 2012). The first policy in question concerns sector specific taxes that will increase rather than decrease distortions and may cause low productivity growth in Hungary; second, flat taxes will not reduce the average labor tax and will not help increase labor force participation; third, overtaxing the financial sector leads to lower growth and slows down the recovery; and fourth, nationalizing private pensions, as well as the invalidation of private contracts by governments increases expropriation risk, undermines property rights, and hence reduce growth (EEAG 2012). However, the Excess Deficit Procedure of the European Union was unable to enforce fiscal discipline in Hungary (EEAG 2012).

On July 6, 2012, Hungary's parliament approved changes to a disputed central bank law, clearing the way to talks with the IMF and EU on a financing backstop which the country needed to cut its high borrowing costs and averts a market crisis (Reuters 2012).

Poland

According to OECD (2010c), Polish macro policy responses to the slowdown were largely appropriate, and the sharp depreciation of the Zloty (Polish currency) cushioned the impact of the foreign shock, however it might result in the postponement of Euro adoption. Since Poland remains outside the Euro zone, its Monetary Policy Council can perform large-scale market interventions. As a result, the exchange rate flexibility at the peak of the crisis had a very positive impact on the Polish export (Plociennik 2012). The slowdown also cooled off inflationary pressure and the labor market adjustment through a rapid slowdown in real wages after hefty increases in 2008 limited employment cutbacks (OECD 2010c). In addition, domestic demand was supported by pre-crisis cuts in taxes and social contributions, infrastructure investments from EU funds, and Poland's hosting of the 2012 European football championships (OECD 2010c).

In 2010, rising demands to fund health care, education, and the state pension system caused the public sector budget deficit to rise to 7.9 % of GDP. In addition, unemployment climbed back to 11.8 %, exceeding the EU average by more than 2 % (CIA 2012). In 2010, due to the global economic slowdown, inflation reached a low of about 2.6 % but afterwards rose to around 3 %, close to the upper limit of the National Bank of Poland's target rate (CIA 2012). Production growth, witnessed since the fourth quarter of 2009, continued at an accelerated rate in 2010 (Piatkowska 2010). In addition to GDP growth, Poland continued its growth and investment in infrastructure across local communities, primarily as a result of EU investment (Reichardt 2011).

Poland's budget deficit grew significantly in 2010, and its government debt reached 55.08 % of the GDP in 2010 (Fig. 2.2). In the first half of 2010 alone, the state budget recorded a deficit of 36.6 billion zloty (compared to a deficit of 16.6 billion zloty for the same period in 2009) (Reichardt 2011). However, effective January 1, 2011, Poland's national Value Added Tax (VAT) rate was increased by one percentage point to 23 % on most consumer goods, including food, electrical appliances, and cosmetics. The tax increase is only temporary, for a period of 3 years ending December 31, 2013 (Reichardt 2011). Raising taxes in the middle of an economic downturn seems counterproductive, as it could inhibit consumer demand, impact inflation, and force Polish consumers to tighten their spending and thus could have a negative effect on the economy. Nevertheless, the rationale of raising the VAT by 1 % for a defined period of time was to aid the public sector finances, provide some assistance to keep public funding commitments, rather than cut programs indiscriminately or adopt brutal austerity programs (Reichardt 2011). The increase in taxes and the budget revenue, by adding an estimated 5 billion zloty a year for the 3 years also aid in Poland's efforts to minimize deficit spending and control public debt. Upon reviewing Poland's financial credibility especially in light of the VAT increase, the IMF announced in October 2010 that it expected to see Poland's deficit-to-GDP ratio to fall below 5 % of the GDP in 2013 (Reichardt 2011).

In addition to its determination to reduce the budget deficit in 2011, the Polish government also announced its intention to enact business-friendly reforms, increase workforce participation, reduce public sector spending growth, lower taxes, and accelerate privatization (CIA 2012). Public pension system reform is another focus of the government after the financial crisis. New legislation aims to change the structure of how cash transfers are managed in the pension system, decreasing cash transfers to private pension funds from 7.3 to 2.3 % (Reichardt 2011). These measures allowed Poland to stay on target in terms of reducing deficit spending and bringing down its budget shortfall (Reichardt 2011). According to estimation, Poland will be the champion in Emerging Europe with a growth of 2.6 % in 2012, and 3.2 % in 2013 (Novinite 2012).

Romania

As the global trade began to revive in 2010, Romania's economy gradually recovered. In 2010, its exports recorded their highest level since 1989 (Boc 2011). Following the formation of a new government, the parliament approved the bailout terms and the IMF unlocked the needed funds afterwards. In February 2010, the IMF disbursed the first tranche of 2.3 billion Euros, with half of the amount helping to plug the budget deficit, and the other half going to the accounts of the central bank (Ban 2010). In March 2010, Romania's credit rating outlook was raised from negative to stable by Standard and Poor's after the IMF resumed a bailout loan to the country and the government passed an austerity budget (Gheorghiu and Gheorghiu 2011; Voinea et al. 2010). In addition, the Fitch Agency rated Romania to the "investment grade" category in July 2011, after the country lost it in 2008 (Boc 2011).

In comparing 2010 to 2009, Romania has a reduction of budget deficit to GDP ratio, from 7.2 to 6.51 %, the trade deficit reduced by about 14 %, and inflation continues its downward trend (Boc 2011; Dobrota 2012). Yet for the same comparison, there was a current account deficit increase of 1.1 % (Dobrota 2012). Drastic austerity measures, as part of Romania's IMF-led agreement led to a further 1.9 % GDP contraction in 2010 and its real GDP growth returned to positive 2.5 % in 2011 as expected (CIA 2012; Global Finance 2012).

According to the Prime Minister of Romania, the government adopted the following measures to reduce the budgetary deficit in 2010 (Boc 2011): a 25 % reduction in public sector wages and a reduction of 173,623 occupied positions in the public sector through the introduction of standard limits on the number of staff in the public administration. In addition, a 15 % reduction in unemployment benefits and children's allowances; the freezing of pensions in 2010 and 2011; the dissolution, merger, and reorganization of 141 governmental agencies; the closure of 67 public hospitals to improve the quality of medical services and to channel financial resources to the remaining more efficient hospitals were employed. Furthermore, receiving both a pension and a salary in the public sector, as well as for pensioners with pensions higher than the average gross salary were prohibited. The elimination of meal and gift vouchers provided to public sector employees and a 50 % reduction in the expenditure ceilings for fuel consumption in public institutions were adopted. The share of staff expenditure in GDP decreased from 9.4 % in 2009 to 7.5 % in 2011 and was expected to reach 7.2 % in 2012. In nominal terms, staff expenditure decreased from 46.8 billion lei (Romanian currency) in 2009 to 40.6 billion lei in 2011 (Boc 2011).

At the same time, there were several measures to increase public revenues, including an increase of the standard VAT rate from 19 to 24 % after the Romanian Constitutional Court rejected the proposal to reduce pensions by 15 % (Boc 2011). Raising the number of contributors to the health insurance system and increasing social insurance contributions by 3.3 % points were also included. In addition, an increase of the tax payable by individuals who own several buildings and transportation vehicles with cylinder capacity exceeds 2000 cm^3 was implemented. An increase of excise duties levied on some alcoholic beverages, cigarettes, gas, and diesel were also important measures. Furthermore, the tax base was broadened by taxing income from interest rates, meal, and gift vouchers. Tax evasion was reduced by imposing strict combating measures.

Romania has been among the best performers in the world in terms of reducing the country risk in the third quarter of 2010 (Gheorghiu and Gheorghiu 2011). The immediate results of the implementation of labor legislation reform were apparent. In just 4 months, after the new legislation went into force (MaySeptember 2011), the number of recorded employment contracts increased by 1,052,331 (out of which 763,698 were active labor contracts; 288,633 labor contracts have ended at the same time). Moreover, even during the economic crisis, the number of active labor contracts exceeded the number in 2008, the year with the highest economic growth in Romania (Boc 2011).

In 2011, Romania came out from the economic recession, having three consecutive quarters of economic growth from the 4th quarter in 2010 to the second quarter in 2011 (Boc 2011). 2011 was the year of maximum growth, which was also the year when excessive deficit policies began. In April 2011, Romania has successfully concluded the first agreement with the international financial aid bodies and started the second agreement without funding, but with the possibility of accessing the funds in case of worsening of the international economic conditions (Boc 2011). With the above measures, Romania ended its past economic model based on consumption and lending, and moved to a growth model focused on investment and jobs (Boc 2011).

In 2011, Romania maintains the highest allotment for investments as a percentage of its GDP, of all EU Member States (Boc 2011). The value of the financial resources allocated for investments increased from 33.8 billion lei in 2010 to 36.06 billion lei in 2011, and 43 billion lei are projected as investments expenditures in 2012. Romania's public debt as percentage of its GDP is one of the lowest in the European Union, about 31.5 % of the GDP in June 2011 (Boc 2011). According to IMF, Romania would see a growth of 1.5 % in 2012 and of 3 % in 2013 (Novinite 2012).

Chapter 5
Future Perspectives and Policy Implications

By the middle of 2012, more than 3 years had passed since the outbreak of the 2008 global financial crisis. Although these five emerging European countries were generally pushed back into a recession due to the economic slowdown in Europe, it is time to reflect upon what had happened during the past few years. Financial crisis triggered economic consequences of inflation, unemployment, drop in purchasing power, growth of public debt as the governments had to devalue national currency or borrow from the International Monetary Fund and others (Terazi and Senel 2011). Although the types of economic crisis, the reasons, and circumstances in different countries in different periods were varied, there are common denominators that can help these countries learn from past mistakes.

Unlike the speedy recoveries of certain Asian economies, such as China and Hong Kong, the situation in these five emerging countries continues to be clouded by significant uncertainties that investors face. Yet, no matter whether a particular country experienced fast or slow recovery, there are lessons to learn by going through the process of various types of structural reforms for short-term consolidation or long-term sustainability. In other words, the economic crisis provided an ideal opportunity to examine the soundness of a nation's economic system and the effectiveness of national governance. In this chapter, we first present the prospects of these five emerging European countries, and then describe their potential challenges in the future. What we describe hereafter is mainly based upon the OECD economic survey report for those countries, supplemented with other relevant reports. The prospects and challenges are meant to provide points of thought or discussion and are not an exhaustive list. This chapter finishes with some policy implications.

Prospects

As of mid-2012, the volatility in Europe continues and the emerging European region remains vulnerable to external factors. However, long-term growth opportunities, including the banking industry in Eastern Europe still exist once the

C. Y.-Y. Lin et al., *National Intellectual Capital and the Financial Crisis in Bulgaria, Czech Republic, Hungary, Romania, and Poland*, SpringerBriefs in Economics,
DOI: 10.1007/978-1-4614-8018-1_5,

turmoil has subsided (Dietz et al. 2012). As a key player in stabilizing the economy, the banking sector needs to tackle the problems of insufficient scale, inefficient operating models, and relatively weak risk and governance processes. If the governments together with the banking sector can learn from the experience of this financial crisis and cope with the new regulations, higher funding and risk costs, and changing customer behavior, the prospects of this region are enormous. The potential of closing the gap between Eastern Europe's economic performance and that of Western Europe provided the impetus for growth in the region. Looking forward, Eastern Europe's development, including the reported five countries are tied closely to other parts of the world. Although these five emerging European countries have not totally recovered from the 2008 global financial crisis and the following recession, with expected rising consumption, trade, investments, and the planned accession of more countries to the European Union and monetary association, this region remains the world's most attractive region for future investments (Ernst and Young 2009).

Bulgaria

Bulgaria has some pre-crisis strengths, structural reforms, and EU financial support that can facilitate its future development. These are briefly listed as follows:

1. Bulgaria maintains its position as one of the countries with high levels of human development and ranks 56th out of 179 countries in the Human Development Index (HDI) in 2008 (Stoilov 2009).
2. It embraced difficult reforms to build macroeconomic stability and stimulate growth. It also built fiscal buffers by accumulating fiscal surpluses between 2004 and 2008, and reduced public debt from over 70 % of its GDP in 2000 to around 16 % in 2010, one of the lowest debt levels in the EU (World Bank 2012).
3. Bulgaria's conservative fiscal policy not only fulfilled the Maastricht requirements, but also contributed to the nation's overall stability (Angelov 2009).
4. Between 2000 and 2010, its average annual growth reached 4.7 %. During that same period, Bulgaria's per capita income as a share of the EU average increased dramatically from 28 to 44 %.
5. In 2012, it remains among the most fiscally disciplined EU member states, which was an important feat in the context of global and European economic uncertainties.
6. To stimulate private sector-led growth, the Government of Bulgaria has placed better roads, rail, and water infrastructure and put an enabling business environment at the top of its agenda.
7. The country also pledged to strengthen the delivery of public services and worked toward ensuring all citizens reap the benefits of growth (World Bank 2012).

8. Under the current EU financial perspective covering the years 2007–2013, Bulgaria has access to approximately US$8.7 billion (€7 billion) in grants (World Bank 2012). It is the only country that is able to sustain its relatively favorable credit ratings, mainly because the efforts of its currency board (Terazi and Senel 2011).
9. Bulgaria provides a wide range of incentives to investors. These include: zero corporate income tax rate for investment in high-unemployment areas; a 2- year VAT exemption for imports of equipment for investment projects over US$6.7 billion (€5 million) that create at least 50 jobs; and depreciation over 2 years for computers and new manufacturing equipment (QFinance 2012a). In addition, foreign and domestic investors are treated equally (Heritage 2012).
10. In the country, there is voice that Bulgaria should try to make the most of the current global crisis by using it as a catalyst to bring needed structural changes to the economy. It had a great chance to reduce the negative effects of the economic crises by using the difficult times to improve its transport and environment infrastructure, and by increasing the efficiency of its economy (Dikov 2009).

The Czech Republic

In the past, the Czech Republic actually profited from downturns in the global economy, as its business costs are lower than those of Germany or France. The country has managed to build up a reputation as being advantageous for services (Ernst and Young 2009). In addition, the country has the following features that may help enhance its future development:

1. Most major state-owned companies have been privatized with foreign participation. There are no restrictions on payments or currency transfers, and residents and non-residents may hold foreign exchange accounts.
2. The government is placing a high priority on fiscal discipline and striving for budgetary balance after years of fiscal deficits (Heritage 2012).
3. The Czech National Bank (CNB) is independent from the government and has both strategic and operational independence in pursuing its only constitutional objective—price stability. Besides the monetary policy, the CNB is also the chief financial regulator in the Czech Republic (Schneider 2009). Moreover, the CNB has been responsible for overseeing banks, capital markets, and insurance and cooperative banking. Such centralized supervision allows for greater information flows, coordinated decisions, and coherent communication (World Bank 2011).
4. The country's free floating exchange rate has functioned as the main absorber of external shocks; it has facilitated the pursuit of an independent and effective monetary policy (IMF 2012b). As a result, IMF rated Czech monetary policy with the inflation-targeting framework appropriate (IMF 2012c).

5. The Czech Republic's financial sector is one of Central and Eastern Europe's most advanced (Heritage 2012), mainly benefitted from a consolidation program and prudential oversight that the central bank initiated in the mid-1990s (World Bank 2011). The Czech Republic has adopted the international standard of Basel II framework (IMF 2008) and established the Financial Market Committee that advises the CNB on supervision strategies, new trends in the financial sector, and supervision practices (World Bank 2011).
6. The legal framework for financial sector supervision was strengthened during the financial crisis (World Bank 2011). In addition, the performance of CNB is very good, mainly with strong capitalization, solid profits, and ample liquidity. Its resilience reflects to a large extent a relatively conservative structure of bank balance sheets, and relatively low indebtedness of the corporate, household sectors, and foreign loans (IMF 2012a; World Bank 2011). The moderate interest rates in the country discouraged households from borrowing in foreign currencies (World Bank 2011).
7. Future prospects of the Czech Republic are promising. During this global financial crisis, despite the FDI downturn, the country remains among the world's twenty most attractive investment destinations. In 2008, it received 5 % more projects than in previous year and for the first time ever, services—including R&D—comprised the majority of new projects, different from past predominated automotive industry (Ernst and Young 2009).
8. The private sector accounts for about 80 % of its GDP and is the main driver of economic growth (Heritage 2012).
9. The Czech Republic government set an ambitious goal of achieving one of the 20 most competitive economies in the world by 2020 (IMF 2012b). Its comprehensive reform strategy outlined concrete plans for developing infrastructure, strengthening institutions and governance, reforming the education sector, further increasing labor market flexibility, and improving the business climate. In addition, export diversification of new products and new markets are also on the agenda.

Hungary

Although most of Hungary's tangible and intangible indicators are in a downward trend, it still has some advantages that can facilitate its future development:

1. Hungary's economic micro-structure underwent rapid modernization in the last two decades. According to the Heritage Foundation (2012), the overall business environment was aided by strong trade freedom, business freedom, property rights, and investment freedom. The rule of law and consistent protection of private property have contributed to Hungary's long-term competitiveness and growth. In addition, Hungary's transparent regulatory framework allows business formation and operation to be efficient and dynamic. The government also

allows 100 % foreign ownership with the exception of some defense-related industries (Heritage 2012).
2. The shift in the tax burden from labor to consumption in 2009 was a positive step toward reducing economic distortion (OECD 2010b).
3. Hungary has concentrated on medium and highly skilled labor and technology, which has made it the leader among transforming economies in terms of technology-based exports (Inotai 2010).
4. The New Hungary Development Plan has a particular focus on SMEs, providing bank guarantees and recapitalization. The plan is based on the availability of US$27.9 billion (€22.4 billion) in EU transfers between 2007 and 2013 (Inotai 2010). Several development programs have also been elaborated within this framework to facilitate the modernization of public administration, growth, employment, competitiveness, environmental protection, education and training, and physical infrastructure development (Inotai 2010).
5. For Hungary, the absence of a major stimulus package may prove to be a medium-term advantage for the rationale that artificial financial injections generally help uncompetitive businesses and sectors to survive (Inotai 2010). In addition, Hungary's financial latitude may be less constrained in the future, as generally the economic stabilization program continues for a period of time after the crisis.
6. Hungary has been most successful in curbing the budget deficit in the region. Even though the 2008 global crisis came unexpectedly, the response was efficient (Terazi and Senel 2011). Effective on 1 January 2012, a new constitution puts a ceiling on the general government debt at 50 % of GDP. If the debt-to-GDP ratio exceeds 50 %, the parliament cannot pass a budget bill for the central government that would lead to an increase in the debt-to-GDP ratio (EEAG 2012).
7. Hungary obtained an IMF financial package of US$25 billion (€20 billion), which is ten times more than the Hungary IMF quota and the biggest international rescue package (about three times) for an emerging market economy. The primary goal of the IMF arrangement was to reduce the increasing stress that ruled in the Hungarian financial markets, while creating the necessary conditions to facilitate the appropriate reforms in Hungary's market intervention and banking sector (Refdahl and Karstensen 2009).
8. During the crisis Hungary has been able to avoid state bankruptcy and a banking system collapse, thus keeping its international credibility. There is demonstrated openness to reform resulting in a decline of the deficit and inflation rates, a restructuring of an outdated social welfare system, and a changing mindset among some sectors (Gurzo and Molnar 2011; Magas 2010).
9. The government has launched a new energy policy to reduce the dependence on Russian energy resources (the Nabucco pipeline) and increase use of bioenergy produced within Hungary (Gurzo and Molnar 2011).

Poland

The objective of Polish economic policy is to create conditions for rapid and sustainable growth, while ensuring the optimal rate of consolidation of public finances, and a high level of structural investments. It also aims at creating an innovative and efficient economy to effectively compete in the global market and use the available resources (Piatkowska 2010). The following features may facilitate the country achieving these goals:

1. Poland has become the largest beneficiary of EU cohesion policy; EU transfers represent an average of 3.3 % of its GDP per year and are expected to raise real growth by an average of 0.5–1.5 % points (OECD 2010c). They provide a unique opportunity for Poland to modernize the economy. In addition, Poland has an easy access to credit and became a direct beneficiary of large-scale aid programs offered by various institutions and governments (Piatkowska 2010). It has been granted, by the World Bank and the European Investment Bank, preferential loans for infrastructure and investment during the crisis (Plociennik 2012).
2. Backed by a law passed in August 2009, the Polish government has launched significant changes in both the systematic and institutional forms of public financing at the sub-national level, aiming at consolidating the public finance system and adding more transparency into the way tax money is spent (Reichardt 2011). In 2009 alone, over 20 amendments were implemented to eliminate unnecessary and contradictory provisions, reduce overregulation, increase freedom of business, and improve public transparency for creating a friendly environment for citizens and entrepreneurs (Piatkowska 2010). In addition, restrictions on capital flows have been removed, and capital markets have become more sophisticated, with the Warsaw Stock Exchange rapidly expanding (Heritage 2012).
3. Poland demonstrated its sound macroeconomic and fundamentals during the financial crisis. It has passed the test that no emergency funding was needed and no private banks were recapitalized by the state, mainly because of its prudential regulation, tight cooperation of the selling of Euro by the Government, and the timely "flexible credit line for stable economies" from the IMF (Kluza, n.d.).
4. In Poland, labor regulation is relatively flexible. Rules on dismissal are quite liberal; however, the employer needs to justify terminations of permanent employment contracts and there is special protection for persons in preretirement age (Plociennik 2012). The flexibility potential is also with wage setting. Only 15 % of employees are members of trade unions, such institutional environment is perfect for foreign corporations investing in Poland (Plociennik 2012).
5. Poland has already set up incentives to encourage working after the retirement age. The old age pension reform launched in the previous decade strongly

supports those willing to continue their professional career despite reaching the retirement age (Plociennik 2012).

6. The reform of higher education started in 2011 should further increase the education efficiency and the R&D quality, linking universities, and the labor market (Plociennik 2012).
7. The Polish currency is considered as highly credible, mainly due to the country's low inflation and the influence of the National Bank of Poland which, many times recently, has shown its independency and determination in defending the monetary value (Plociennik 2012).
8. Large banks were not interested in risky foreign transactions, and acting in a conservative manner, focused mainly on financing infrastructure and low risk business projects in Poland (Plociennik 2012). In addition, the active Polish Financial Supervision Authority helps strengthen the bank performance and reduce risk through monitoring and published recommendations.
9. Poland pursues its policies under the Maastricht regime, adhering to the budget deficit 3 % of GDP limit (Plociennik 2012). By Polish law, if the public debt reaches above 55 % of the GDP, legal requirements force Polish officials to begin automatic cuts in public spending (Reichardt 2011).
10. The strength of Poland is a large and diversified sector of locally oriented family businesses. They create a relatively stable environment for employment thus reduces external impact. Its exporting sector is also diversified, free from the threat of a dominate industry failure (Plociennik 2012). In addition, Poland's increasingly competitive financial system and low corporate tax rates have spurred private-sector dynamism (Heritage 2012).
11. Privatization of the economy moved at a quick pace. In 1989, 53 % of the workforce was employed in the public sector. By 2002, only 26 % of the Polish workforce was in the public sector (Reichardt 2011).
12. In November 2009, the Polish Council of Ministers has mapped the country's medium-term as well as long-term development within the time horizon of 2030. Nine implementation strategies were prepared, including strategy for Innovativeness and Efficiency of the Economy, Developing Human Resources, Developing Transport, Energy Security and the Environment, Efficient State, Developing Social Capital, Regional Development, Security Strategy for the Republic of Poland, and Sustainable Development of Rural Areas and Agriculture (Piatkowska 2010).

Romania

From NIC development indicators, Romania is improving despite the severe impact of the financial crisis. The following features may facilitate its future development:

1. Romania has been a fast-growing member of the European Union and NATO. The government has been implementing economic reforms that are consistent with the Maastricht criteria. Macroeconomic improvements have spurred the growth of the middle class and helped reduce poverty (Heritage 2012; Voinea et al. 2010).
2. An important factor that contributed to higher economic growth in Romania was the pronounced dynamics of labor productivity (Zamfir 2010). Although it decreased in 2009 when reported per person employed, labor productivity per hour worked improved even in the times of crisis (Voinea et al. 2010).
3. Romania has concluded a financing agreement for a 2–year total loan of US$27.1 billion (€20 billion) with the IMF, EU, EBRD, and World Bank, under the conditions of reducing the budget deficit and freezing wages in the public sector (Zaman and Georgescu 2009).
4. The Prime Minister of Romania regards the global economic crisis as an opportunity for profound reforms, despite its negative economic and social consequences. The government has implemented various types of reforms, including the state apparatus, the governmental agencies, public sector employees' wages, public pension system, labor legislation, social dialogue, education system, healthcare system, social assistance, legal system, and fiscal framework (Boc 2011). Such structural reforms will have positive impact on the development of the country for decades (Boc 2011).
5. From this financial crisis, the country has learned that they must leave populism with rash policies that deplete public financial resources (such as generous social programs) behind. Instead, the government should have realistic public policies with financial support for the country's medium and long-term development (Boc 2011).
6. The Romanian banking sector proved to be resilient in this financial crisis. Without the need for bailouts, the country's (foreign-owned) banks reported even higher profits in 2009 than in 2008 (Ban 2010). Its gross fixed capital formation (business investment) also reached higher than EU average levels, even in 2009.
7. Romania remains attractive to foreign investors, largely because the crisis reduced the wage expectations of Romania's skilled and adaptable labor force. Boosted by cash-for-clunkers programs in Germany and France, the exports of the Romanian car manufacturer Dacia and of its numerous suppliers continued to grow (Ban 2010). To boost foreign investment, the government established the Agency for Foreign Investment in 2004. In addition to advertising Romania as an attractive investment destination, the country strengthens its tax administration, enhances transparency, and creates legal means to resolve contract disputes quickly. Romania's accession to the European Union in 2007 has also helped improve the investment environment (QFinance 2010b).
8. Romania's fertile arable land, vibrant oil and gas industry, and well-educated workforce (there are more than 50,000 specialists in information technology) have attracted high levels of foreign direct investment (FDI) (QFinance 2012b).

9. Romania has a higher share of renewable energy sources (RES) in total consumption, and the trend is increasing (11.86 % in 2007 compared to 9.95 % in 2003). The government also commits to a 24 % RES target for 2020 (Voinea et al. 2010).

Challenges

Although the governments of these five emerging European countries have strategized to cope with the debt crisis and implemented required structural reforms for future sustainability, many challenges remain to be tackled. Especially, most Eastern European economies continue to rely on European fiscal transfers. To construct a more resilient economy, these countries need to considerably step up their efforts in industrial and innovation policies (Kattel 2010). This section briefly introduces the issues observed that need special attention for each of the countries.

Bulgaria

1. For future national development, Bulgaria needs to strengthen the efficiency of public spending by vigorously implementing the planned structural reforms in the area of public administration, healthcare, education, and pensions in order to boost productivity and ensure sustainable convergence within the European Union (European Union 2010).
2. Bureaucracy and corruption in the public administration, a weak and slow-moving judiciary, and the presence of organized crime remain significant challenges and deter investment (CIA 2012; Heritage 2012). One weakness of the Bulgarian institutional context is the lack of a system for monitoring and assessing of institutions' efficiency and effectiveness. Such deficiency and the hidden economy foster corruption and the criminalization of the economy, thus hindering the functioning of market mechanisms (Nonchev et al. 2011).
3. Bulgaria's progress toward the Millennium Development Goals (MDG) has been accompanied by greater inequalityand exclusion, because about 10 % of the population account for 40 % of the country's income and expenditure. This proportion is exacerbated by deteriorating quality and rising costs in the basic education and health care, which leads to even greater inequality of opportunities. In particular, low incomes, low educational levels, and limited access to health services have brought about serious social disadvantages of some regions and ethnic groups (Social Watch 2010).
4. Bulgaria's aid management system lacks transparency. Information about aid decision-making is not available to the general public, and it is extremely difficult to find out anything about aid flows (Social Watch 2010).

5. The negative aspects of licensing makes bribery a cheaper and faster way of doing business, which is reinforced by the inefficiency of the judicial system. Even though the government implemented two waves of reducing the regulatory burden, that process failed to bring about a tangible reduction of corruption (Nonchev et al. 2011).
6. There is no constant and efficient dialogue between the government and businesses, such a dialogue would have contributed to the development of more effective institutions (Nonchev et al. 2011).

The Czech Republic

1. The Czech Republic needs to strengthen its public finance management, plans for its rapidly aging population through a sustainable pension and health care system (CIA 2012; IMF 2008). The country's ratio of age-related spending to GDP is projected to rise by 6.4 % points over the period to 2060, mainly in the areas of health care and pensions (OECD 2010a). Instituting partial indexation of the retirement age to life expectancy, increasing labor force participation among groups with high social benefits, as well as policies to boost labor supply, such as migration policy should be considered (OECD 2010a).
2. Slow legislative and judicial reform, uneven contract enforcement, bureaucracy, property rights infringement, and corruption are obstacles to foreign investment (CIA 2012; Heritage 2012). Therefore, a more efficient and business friendly environment needs to be established. Currently, regulatory bottlenecks and lack of transparency remain burdensome, licensing and bankruptcy processes are lengthy and costly, and company registration is controlled by the courts and can be slow and complicated (Heritage 2012).
3. Although the Czech government has drawn up a comprehensive reform strategy, implementation of these plans requires sustained efforts (IMF 2012b). In particular, there is evidence that a substantial share of public spending in the Czech Republic is inefficient (OECD 2010a). Therefore, consolidation plans and future development should place greater emphasis on the expenditure side of the budget.
4. The country should adopt a structural indicator of the budget balance, increase the transparency of its fiscal policy, and implement unified accounting and real time financial management to further streamline its public expenditure (OECD 2010a).
5. A review of social spending should be undertaken, with particular attention to whether some benefits that are not income tested should be phased out at higher incomes (OECD 2010a).
6. Policy continuity and coordinated efforts across the divisions between government ministries and between central, regional, and municipal authorities are needed. The independence of individual ministries and the lack of a strong

institutional center capable of ensuring unity in approach and consistency in implementation become a particular challenge in the process of regulatory reform and fiscal consolidation (OECD 2010a).

7. Czech banks have a surprisingly high return on equity (26.4 % in 2009), indicating that they might be too profitable, at the cost of consumers. In addition, their current ratios of highly liquid assets to total assets may not be enough to meet new Basel III liquidity regulations (World Bank 2011).
8. The modularity in restructured industry production leads to lower value added activities with reduced domestic linkages. In addition, banking sector transformative change also breaks the ties with domestic productive sector and increase inflow of cross-border lending. This led to loss of competitiveness through low productivity growth and through currency appreciations (Kattel 2010).

Hungary

By the end of 2011, Hungary was one of the most financially vulnerable countries in Europe outside the Euro area (EEAG 2012). For Hungary, boosting potential growth calls for continued structural reforms in labor market, education, entrepreneurship, and innovation (OECD 2010b). The following challenges provide some thinking points for the country's future development:

1. The 2008 global financial crisis exposed several weaknesses in the Hungary's supervisory framework, thus fiscal consolidation and better management of public finance are needed (Horvath 2009; Inotai 2010). Areas of improvement include attaching higher costs for risky lending, transparent financial products disclosure, and close cooperation between the central bank and the supervisory authority (OECD 2010b). Hungary's public administration is also one of the least efficient among OECD and accession countries (OECD 2010b). Hungary's central and sub-national workers account for a relatively high percentage (20 %) of total domestic employment with low total activity ratio (OECD 2010b). To help maintain public administration reform with expected results, the government should establish a unit with a mandate to both promote and assess reform progress (OECD 2010b).
2. Hungarian economic deterrents include bureaucracy, inadequate judicial capacity, and a nontransparent investment code. The courts are slow and severely overburdened, thus a final ruling on a contract dispute can take more than a year (Heritage 2012). In addition, tax evasion in Hungary is widespread and morally acceptable (Horvath 2009).
3. School efficiency should be raised. For example, vocational school training does not adequately prepare people for the labor market. The proportion of adults with tertiary qualifications is low. The country should improve incentives to provide tertiary studies that match labor market needs, especially in science (OECD 2010b). Hungary has by far the lowest proportion of science

graduates among OECD countries. The authorities should continue to prioritize the allocation of finance to subject areas conducive to innovation and thus economic growth (OECD 2010b).

4. Hungary's rigid labor market, one of the lowest levels of activity rate among the OECD countries and a very high level of officially unemployed young people without sufficient education (Heritage 2012; Inotai 2010). Its labor force participation is significantly lower than in other countries, such as Poland (EEAG 2012). Only 57 % of people between 19 and 64 had a legal job in Hungary in 2009 (OECD 2009). The average effective retirement age in Hungary was about 2.5 years lower than the legal age, thus lowering the participation rate (EEAG 2012).
5. Although with the highest share of private spending on health in the EU, the Hungarian health care system does not deliver adequate outcomes by international standards. For example, the health status of the Hungarian population is among the poorest in the OECD with low life expectancy (OECD 2010b).
6. Hungarian Parliament passed the Fiscal Responsibility Act in 2008, establishing an independent Fiscal Council. However, in April 2010, it was abolished and replaced with a new body. Without independent forecasts and analyses, it is impossible for the new council to provide the fiscal transparency and evaluation of sustainability that the original council was able to (EEAG 2012).
7. Unlike the Czech Republic, Poland, and Slovakia, which used the loans for boosting exports and competitiveness, in Hungary the loans were used mainly for consumption purposes (Bocian and Sadowski 2008), thus delayed its national development.
8. Hungary implemented some bad economic policies, thus the development of the Hungarian economy was slow between 2002 and 2006 (Gurzo and Molnar 2011; Terazi and Senel 2011). For example, the public sector including education, health care, the overstaffed and inefficient state, and local governments had a 50 % pay raise without economic basis, causing a high deficit year by year starting in 2002 (Gurzo and Molnar 2011). In addition, Hungary had 750,000 foreign currency mortgage loans in Hungary worth a total of US$24.2bn (HUF4, 500 bn), over 90 % of which are made in Swiss Francs (OECD 2010c). Furthermore, Hungary keeps an overstretched and too generous social benefit system. As a result, the necessary reforms in the economy, society, and the administration were delayed; waste, corruption, and "white collar crime" were growing in size and frequency (Gurzo and Molnar 2011; Inotai 2010). However, the government's intended reforms faced a lot of social conflicts with various social groups (Gurzo and Molnar 2011).
9. Hungarian government's rapid loss of credibility and the equally rapid increase of the opposition's populism and demagoguery have led to a large majority of the population voted against all reforms in March 2008 (Inotai 2010). In Hungary, the very high level of demagoguery, populism, and short-term interests has served as a mental barrier to implementing an efficient anti-crisis plan, which became an even bigger political and psychological obstacle

to clear in the postcrisis situation (Inotai 2010). The opposition's misuse of democratic institutions and unexpected interaction with international actors (including the IMF and the European Union) has caused the suspension of IMF financial aid (Inotai 2010).

10. Hungary should enhance its export, diversify export markets, and deepen the current industries' capacity for value-added and technology-incorporating products and activities (Gurzo and Molnar 2011; Inotai 2010).
11. Hungary carries an over regulated and not enterprise-friendly economy, causing companies to flee to the black market or leave the country (Gurzo and Molnar 2011).

Poland

Although Poland had an outstanding performance during this financial crisis, it still has the following challenges to tackle:

1. For longer term development, Poland's infrastructure needs to be modernized, especially its transportation and broadband Internet (CIA 2012; OECD 2010c). Broadband Internet is insufficiently developed mainly due to the control maintained by the incumbent operator and the inability of the regulator to ensure effective competition in the market (OECD 2010c). Downsizing public ownership, easing regulation in retail distribution and professional services, and building a business-friendly environment are also important (CIA 2012; OECD 2010c).
2. Formalities to start up a business, get construction permits and register properties are excessive, risking corruption to get around them (OECD 2010c). In addition, an inefficient commercial court system, a rigid labor code, bureaucratic red tape, burdensome tax system, and persistent low-level corruption continues to keep the private sector from its full potential (CIA 2012; Heritage 2012; World Bank 2010).
3. Cuts in the tax wedge during the financial crisis were not totally compensated and thus initially procyclical (OECD 2010c).The accumulation of large fiscal deficits in recent years runs the risk of undermining Poland's long-term competitiveness and highlights the need for more disciplined management of public finance (Heritage 2012). In the most recent year, total government expenditures, including consumption and transfer payments, increased slightly to 43.3 % of GDP (Heritage 2012). The creation of an independent fiscal council to monitor and assess the implementation would enhance the overall credibility of the fiscal framework (OECD 2010c).
4. Health care reform can include reallocating resources from the hospital sector into both primary care and long term care, providing hospitals with clear incentives to rationalize the use of financial resources, and streamlining

responsibilities between the National Health Fund and central and local governments (OECD 2012d).

5. Poland benefits from EU transfers—an average of 3.3 % of its GDP per year; however, absorbing them efficiently and managing the macroeconomic repercussions effectively will be a challenge (Reichardt 2011).
6. The country needs to prepare for the Euro adoption. Developing the capacity to stabilize the economy once monetary and exchange rate policies are abandoned is the priority (OECD 2010c). In Poland, commercial banks control nearly 90 % of assets, and majority foreign-owned banks account for two-thirds of that amount (Heritage 2012). Therefore, the soundness of the bank system needs to be monitored.
7. An analysis of the Polish general budget receipts shows that Poland's revenue has increased markedly over the last 10 years. However, when taken into account the funding from EU sources, the level of public revenue displays a leveling starting in 2007 (Reichardt 2011). As EU funding will discontinue someday, Poland needs to build up its own economic strength as soon as possible.
8. Future challenges for Poland include: enhancing public sector efficiency, cutting tax expenditures, broadening the tax base, opting for less distortive taxes, reforming property taxes, introducing a carbon tax, reforming the farmers' social security system, removing pension privileges for selected occupations, continued tightening of eligibility criteria for disability support, and raising and equalizing retirement ages for men and women (OECD 2010c; 2012d).
9. Broad structural reforms are needed to benefit more extensively from globalization. The role of the state should be reduced through a transparent process of privatization and a faster removal of administrative burdens (OECD 2012c). However, the country also needs to attend to the issue of massive unemployment incurred by fast privatization (Reichardt 2011).
10. Since 2005, the minimum wage in Poland has increased by 14 % relative to the average wage, which exceeds the OECD average (OECD 2010c). Policy makers should refrain from raising further the minimum-to-average wage ratio (OECD 2010c). On the other hand, Poland has a surplus of poorly qualified labor and a shortage of highly qualified workforce. Only 1/3 of graduates from lower secondary schools continued their education at higher vocational schools (Plociennik 2012). The main reason for such situation is a relatively low flexibility of Polish education and salary systems, which respond rather slowly to structural mismatch (Piatkowska 2010).
11. Poland invests a low share in R&D (approximately 0.6 % of its GDP) and the innovativeness of Polish economy is low (Piatkowska 2010). In 2007 the patenting rate in Poland was 3.82 per one million inhabitants while the average for the EU27 was 116.54 (Plociennik 2012). Lack of effective cooperation between universities and businesses is a serious economic weakness (Plociennik 2012). More support for commercial R&D, better

matching between demand and supply for skills and greater competition between higher education institutions are needed (Piatkowska 2010).
12. For cutting greenhouse gas emissions, integrating the Polish electricity market with its neighbors' would help spread climate change efforts more efficiently. Poland is increasing the production of nuclear power and natural gas; however, the country should take the tail risks and the short- and long-term environmental costs into account (OECD 2012d).

Romania

Although Romania has good improvement in both tangible and NIC indicators, it still faces the following challenges:

1. Corruption and red tape continue to handicap the Romanian business environment and judicial and legislative unpredictability remains a significant problem (CIA 2012; QFinance 2012b).
2. Its budget deficit has been on the rise, putting greater pressure on the government for fiscal restraint (Heritage 2012). The weak capacity of Romanian central and municipal public administration makes it difficult to launch ambitious public works programs (Ban 2010).
3. The country needs to greatly enhance its infrastructure. Almost half of its extensive rail (the fourth largest in Europe) functions only at half capacity and about two-thirds of its national roads are in need of long overdue repairs (Ban 2010). The modernization, refurbishment of new production capacity, and computerization of Romanian society, including rural areas, are also required for national development (Zamfir 2010)
4. Romanian living standards are among the lowest in the EU (Gheorghiu and Gheorghiu 2011). Only about 60 % of the rural population can connect to potable water and sewage systems (Ban 2010).
5. Unlike other European governments taking austerity measures, the Romanian government did not have political support from the opposition for any measure of budgetary austerity and of structural reform of the state. The Parliament brought more than 9 impeachment actions against the government between 2009 and 2010 (Boc 2011)
6. In Romania, the absence of a long-term state development strategy and the lack of a competent state administration accounts for the fact that the country absorbed barely 10 % of the available EU structural funds during the first 3 years of EU membership. By contrast, other postcommunist EU member states absorbed 25–34 % of available EU funds during the same period. The size of the lost opportunities is an astonishing 30,000 jobs per year (Ban 2010). The low usage of EU funding, since 2007 only 4.8 % of the 4.3 billion Euros allocated for employment programs, was reportedly caused by the public servants' fear of judicial harassment (Ban 2010).

7. In 2010, more than 4 million Romanians were not employed—at least not in Romania and not in the formal economy (Voinea et al. 2010).
8. Although the country has an oversupply of Western-educated specializations demanded by the civil service, the central government, and municipalities have had a spotty record of integrating young talent into their ranks (Ban 2010).
9. Romania envisages Euro adoption in 2015, which is less than 3 years for resolving its macroeconomic imbalances (Voinea et al. 2010). In addition, curbing inflation is a key requirement to switch its currency to the Euro (QFinance 2012b). Repayment of the IMF loan in the years ahead could create strains in the foreign exchange market if fiscal policy is not sustainable and macroeconomic stability is still uncertain (Voinea et al. 2010).
10. Romania has a low investment in R&D, only 0.58 % in 2008 and 0.2 % of the GDP in 2009, compared to the EU goal of 3 % set by the Lisbon Agenda. Moreover, public funds for research are used ineffectively, as they fail to create a spreading out effect in the private sector. In addition, there is a weak link between academic research and industrial applications (Voinea et al. 2010). Therefore, attending to these issues are important (Zamfir 2010).
11. Romania has made significant environmental improvements in the last 5–6 years, aiming at the Europe 2020 Strategy of "20/20/20" targets by reducing 20 % gas emissions against the base year, reaching a 20 % share of renewable sources in total energy consumption, and increasing energy efficiency by 20 % (Voinea et al. 2010). However, the country is still employing 4 times more energy to produce a unit of GDP compared to EU average and the urban population is exposed to one of the highest air pollution conditions in the European Union (Voinea et al. 2010).
12. Romania has a very high degree of income inequality. Part of it can be explained by the flat tax (16 %) fiscal policy (Voinea et al. 2010).

Policy Implications

The main cause for the recession of these five emerging European countries is their high integration with the European economies, inefficient public financial management, and unsustainable polices in some countries. Sound public administration will require a transparent financial system, harmonized accounting, a robust and independent regime for monitoring fiscal targets, good public assets management, and effective national governance. These characteristics manifest that intangibles—people, systems, and governance—are the key success factors. National intellectual capital (NIC) represents national intangible assets. Research results reported in this booklet provide valuable information for the policy makers to look back on the national intangibles before the crisis, observe their co-development with the GDP during and after the crisis, and then draw lessons from it.

By investigating economic development and NIC development from 2005 to 2010, we have been able to connect the coevolution of tangibles and intangibles for the reported emerging European countries. Implications that can be drawn from our research findings are as follows:

First, national intellectual capital development goes together with the economic development and should be regarded as an enhancer of economic growth. The co-development of NIC and GDP with a high positive correlation (Fig. 3.7) indicates the higher the national intellectual capital the higher the GDP. That is, from our data of 48 countries, the intangible national intellectual capital development goes together with GDP growth. Figures 3.8, 3.9, 3.10, 3.11 and 3.12 further show that NIC development reflects the economic changes of these five countries during the financial crisis. Most of the NIC individual capitals decline, including the most advanced country in this cluster—The Czech Republic, except Poland. Such findings agree with the economic development in these countries during the financial crisis. Poland's outstanding economic performance is clearly seen from its continuous advancement of NIC, human capital, market capital, and process capital (Figs. 3.8, 3.9, 3.10, and 3.11). On the contrary, the negative effect of Hungary's political instability is reflected in its water-shed slide of short-term NIC—market capital and process capital (Fig. 3.15) started 2006. Therefore, attending to the development of NIC should help policy makers gain different perspectives on economic growth and identify some early signs for timely national strategies.

Second, achieving financial independence should have a time table, as EU and IMF financial aid will stop someday. All these five countries rely on external EU and IMF funding to support national development. Their short-term NIC market capital and process capital progress before the financial crisis demonstrated their investment in international trade and infrastructure building. However, the short-term NIC is also susceptible to external shock, as exhibited in Fig. 3.15. Since external EU and IMF financial aid will stop someday, the countries need to develop self-support mechanism or industries for future development. Besides, Eastern European economies are experiencing decreasing returns from integration into European production networks as they still seriously lag European core economies and East Asian catching up countries both in productivity and knowledge intensity (Kattel 2010). Their very low renewal capital and slow improvement over the years (Fig. 3.12) provides a direction for the countries to plan a mid-term balance between the external aid and internal support for their long-term sustainability. In addition, most of the banks in these five countries are foreign-owned (some over 90 % such as the Czech Republic and Romania). Such a financial system structure is prone to external impact as well. During this financial crisis, luckily through the assistance of the IMF, foreign banks agreed not to withdraw money from their East European subsidiaries, thus stabilize the economy of these countries. When dealing with any form of capital flow, the government must strike a balance between encouraging financial FDI, its monitoring, and managing macro prudential risks (World Bank, n.d.). At least an establishment of a cross-border deposit guarantee scheme should be a precondition.

Third, synergy between the new and the old system is critical for a successful transformation from central planning to market economy. All these five countries were under a communist regime with a cumbersome public sector, generous social welfare, and an ineffective public system. In the market economy system, efficiency, transparency, convenience, and business-friendly environment are required. In good days, the problems of losing competitiveness through wage hike or unsustainable policies do not pose threats to the countries. However, in bad times, these problems surfaced to the level of requiring consolidation or austerity as the case in this financial crisis. Oftentimes, the needed reforms receive strong resistance and public protests by interest groups and slowdown national development. The two political unstable and NIC declining countries in this country cluster—Bulgaria and Hungary had a relatively large scale human capital ranking lost (Figs. 3.17 and 3.21), reflecting losing human capital international competitiveness and global competitiveness (Fig. 1.1). The old systems are not necessarily bad (such as social benefits), they only need to be modified to fit the market value and become sustainable. Another example is Romonian, well-educated young talents were not fully integrated into the civil service system to upgrade the public administration. Therefore, the synergy between the old and new systems needs to be pursued for advancing to developed economy in this region.

Fourth, more effective national and NIC governance systems need to be established, such as over regulation and corruption. A common complaint in these five countries is bureaucracy, corruption, over regulation, and inefficient public administration. International organizations, such as the OECD, IMF, and World Bank all suggest their aggressive public sector reforms. One good example is Romania only absorbed about 10 % of the available EU structural funds during the first 3 years of EU membership, which is equivalent to the loss of 30,000 jobs per year. In addition, since 2007 the country only used 4.8 % of the money allocated by EU for employment programs, just because of public servants' fear of judicial harassment after approval of the EU projects (Ban 2010). It is the resistance of responsibility and the failure of the surveillance system. Therefore, national governance system needs to be designed and effectively implemented. In addition, setting up a NIC governance system by continuously monitoring NIC development should also help detect early warning signs of potential risk. For example, Bulgaria has a very low government debt of less than 20 %, even during the financial crisis. However, its GDP growth is low and unemployment is high. Its NIC development and global competiveness (rated by the World Economic Forum) all show downgrade trend. Therefore, economic indicator is not enough to examine the healthiness of a country. NIC governance system help reveal early signs of decline as reported in this volume.

Fifth, visionary and responsible public servants need to be cultivated and experts need to be involved with national development. From the economic background of these five countries, it is clear that Poland's outstanding performance during this financial crisis has good reasons. While its neighboring countries were using EU funding to support public sector wage raise, generous social benefits and consumption, Poland used the money to modernize the country;

implement public finance, education and pension reforms; and to raise productivity and growth. During the financial crisis, Poland was a rare country that raised taxes in the middle of a downturn and at the same time cutting a large number of public sector employees (Reichardt 2011). Such policies could easily backfire, yet the Polish decision makers had the courage to carry their responsibility in curbing the rise of public debt and budget deficits. In addition, the country has already mapped its nine long-term strategies for national development and well-being. The country has visionary and responsible leaders and really implemented the plans. NIC development of Poland fully supports its economic performance. As Figs. 3.8, 3.9, 3.10, and 3.11 indicated, Poland is rapidly narrowing its gap with Hungary. If the course stays the same with Hungary continuing to have political strife and Poland steadily progressing toward its goal, its surpassing Hungary is only a matter of time. In addition, experts can be involved for better national development. Financial sector in the Czech Republic is very advanced among the Central and East European countries, partially because the country has an independent Financial Market Committee to provide timely suggestions and advice to stay in tune with the national development and to build a more resilient national financial system.

Sixth, strategies between focus and diversification need to be weighed for effective national and NIC development. A key source of economic slowdown in this region is the over reliance on export to EU countries. The drastic production drop in the Czech Republic is caused by reducing demand from its dominate autoindustry. On the contrary, Poland weathered the crisis pretty well partially because it did not have a single dominate industry. In addition, Poland spent efforts to expand its local market rather than totally relied on exports. This region is still developing and has promising prospects. However, whether they can achieve the level of their western partners depends on their strategies after this financial crisis. Therefore for long-term development, discussion about national strategy needs to be conducted as early as possible, taking into account NIC development.

Seventh, investment in research and development is the key source of future competitiveness for these emerging European countries. Our 3D NIC development trajectory unveils impeding factors to GDP growth for these five countries, summarized in Table 3.3. Frequency count indicates that R&D-related impeding factors has the largest total count of 14, followed by market capital and human capital-related issues of 12 and 10 counts, respectively. In addition, Table 3.4 indicates five each efficiency drivers to achieve the targeted GDP, benchmarking Germany. Surprisingly, out of the total 25 efficiency drivers of the five countries, 18 are R&D-related issues, including basic research, business R&D, patents, and university-enterprise cooperation. Figure 3.12 shows that renewal capital of these countries (except the Czech Republic) largely positioned at the lower part of the 48-country landscape, representing low R&D and innovation comparing with world major countries. In addition, their R&D % of GDP is generally much lower than EU suggested 3 %. Besides, more technology-based export to increase added value is also suggested for this region. Therefore, to achieve the level of Germany, these countries should target for increasing their R&D and renewal capital as the goal of their next stage development.

Eighth, to speed-up future Euro currency adoption, continuous structural reform is essential. Entering the Euro zone is the goal of these countries, provided that Euro sustains this crisis. To be admitted to the zone, certain criteria need to be met including the public deficit less than 3 %, government debt less than 60 % of the GDP, and so on. Much concern is on the unsustainable pension system and health care system with the population aging. In addition, the over stretching social welfare also adds burden to public finance. Therefore, a comprehensive scale of structural reform is needed in order to achieve the goal in the specified timeframe, such as 2015 planned by the Romanian government. In line with the above suggestion to involve experts, creating independent national councils of various kinds, such as R&D and public finance management committee, should help the countries keep their development on track.

Concluding Remark and Emerging Insights

In the wake of the 2008 global financial crisis, speed of recovery varies in different parts of the world. In late 2012, economic growth worldwide was slowing down. The growth in international trade has been disappointing, mostly due to a sharp decline in Eurozone imports. In emerging economies, such as China, India and Brazil, production growth is also slowing down due to both a reduction in export and lower domestic spending. For the United States, growth was expected to increase slightly to 2.25 % in 2012 and 2013. Global international trade was expected to recover to a certain extent in 2013. The economy of these five countries experienced another slowdown due to EU region was still mired in the sovereign debt trouble.

Although significant steps have already been taken by EU authorities to tighten financial regulations and rebalance economies, it is a difficult and prolonged process with a large scale of imbalances. According to research, reducing public debt to precrisis levels will constrain government expenditures for at least a decade (Schwab 2011) and on average, it takes four and a half years to get back to the same per capita GDP where a country started out and about the same amount of time for unemployment to stop rising (Rogoff 2011).

As a recap, to counter worsening economic conditions worldwide, a total of US$2 trillion in stimulus packages, amounting to approximately 3 % of the world gross domestic product, has been allocated (some of the packages include measures that extend into subsequent years), an amount that exceeds the call by the International Monetary Fund (IMF) for fiscal stimulus totaling 2 % of global GDP. IMF also estimated that as of January 2009, the U.S. fiscal stimulus packages as a percentage of the GDP in 2009 would amount to 1.9 %, for the Euro area 0.9 %, for Japan 1.4 %, for Asia excluding Japan 1.5 %, and for the rest of the G-20 countries 1.1 % (Nanto 2009).

This global financial crisis came with unexpected speed. Although there were early signs of problems in public statistics, they were largely neglected by countries seriously in trouble, such as Greece. When the financial crisis hit, some deficit countries faced the combined problems of a sharp contraction in private demand, an impaired financial system and weak public finances, which overwhelmed the governments in deep trouble.

After this financial crisis, a new surveillance mechanism is in place to initiate necessary procedure and to propose economic sanctions on a member state whose structural imbalances are not corrected. Important legislative changes are also underway at EU level to improve the surveillance of imbalances and to help ensure that the necessary corrective action is undertaken where risks emerge (Barnes 2010). Alongside with planned structural reforms, macroeconomic, financial, and fiscal management would be strengthened in an integrated way in order to reap the best result (Barnes 2010). Some countries have also been experimenting with creating an independent fiscal council to monitor and assess official fiscal projections. Furthermore, structural reform efforts were made to use more output-based performance measures and to choose the measures with care to avoid distorting incentives.

With the goal of joining the Euro zone in the near future, these five emerging European countries need to adhere to the regulations and criteria set by the European Union. For meeting the goal and continuous economic development, the principle recommended by the Chairman of Polish Financial Supervision Authority is a useful roadmap. He said, there are "four pillars of sound economic policy during economic expansion: public finances under control, long-term monetary policy conducted by an independent central bank, conservative prudential supervision performed by an integrated and independent authority, and firm deposit guarantee scheme" (Kluza, n.d.). In addition, the three main directions of the Europe 2020 Strategy: smart growth, sustainable growth, and inclusive growth (Voinea et al. 2010) also provide an excellent guideline for the countries reported in this volume to map their mid-term and long-term strategies.

In terms of future NIC development, our other study on the top ten NIC ranking countries reveals that the interplay among the four capitals—human capital, market capital, process capital, and renewal capital—resulted in the best synergetic prospect for GDP growth. When their weaker capital (process capital) interacts with stronger capital (market capital), both effects on the GDP are enhanced (Lin 2011). This finding prompts our suggestion for the five countries to cultivate visionary and responsible public officers, involve experts from universities and industries to form independent national councils of various types for a joint effort of effective national development and well-being.

Overall, NIC intelligence suggests that in an era when the intangible asset has become a key competitive advantage, investing in national intellectual capital development is investing in future economic development and national well-being.

Appendix 1
Summary of the Main Stimulus Packages of the Five East European Countries

C. Y.-Y. Lin et al., *National Intellectual Capital and the Financial Crisis in Bulgaria, Czech Republic, Hungary, Romania, and Poland*, SpringerBriefs in Economics,
DOI: 10.1007/978-1-4614-8018-1,

Country	Date	Amount	Item and remarks
Bulgaria	January 21, 2009	#1 (reference number) US$3.7bn (BGN5.6bn)	The government secured US$3.7bn (BGN5.6bn) of investment spending in the budget
	June 28, 2009	#2	Bulgaria provided a US$32.9mn (BGN50mn) credit line to the shipbuilding and ship repair sectors
		US$32.9mn (BGN50mn)	The money would come from the state budget and would be managed by the Bulgarian Development Bank (BDB)
			The package also benefits tourism mainstay in Bulgaria
The Czech Republic	November 10, 2008	#3	The Czech Republic has fared well through the financial crisis and the situation did not require drastic or emergency measures, as domestic banks have significant liquidity and sufficient capital to cover risks
		US$63,630 (CZK1.26mn)	The Czech government approved a proposal for increasing the insurance of deposits in banks up to US$63,630 (CZK1.26mn)
	February 16, 2009	#4 US$3.3bn (CZK72bn)	The proposed stimulus package—a total of US$3.3bn (CZK72bn), or 1.9 % of its GDP, has US$1.8bn (CZK40bn) in new corporate tax cuts that equal 1.1 % of GDP
	April 8, 2009	#5 US$1.99bn (CZK40bn)	The Czech Republic's main political parties agreed to a US$1.99bn (CZK40bn) package of economic stimulus
	2008–2010	#6 Fiscal packages US$6,500mn	Stimulus package as 0.2 % of 2008 GDP
Hungary	November 13, 2008	#7	US$6.5bn (HUF 1.4tn) in direct subsidies to Hungarian companies in 2009 and 2010—much of it from a restructuring of EU funding
		US$6.5bn (HUF 1.4tn)	Among which, US$2.3bn (HUF500bn) were available to companies under the New Hungary Development Plan and another US$1.9bn (HUF400bn) were available under the New Hungary Rural Development Program
		US$8.4bn (HUF 1.8tn)	The package also covered 2,300 exporting SMEs in the form of direct subsidies, loan guarantees, and interest subsidies
			The EU development funding supported US$8.4bn (HUF 1.8tn) for Hungary's construction industry
			Companies that maintained their staff numbers got discounts on payroll taxes
			Hungarian government drew EU money and Workforce Fund to support the stimulus package
	April 19, 2009	#8 budget cut	Hungarian government cut back state expenditures by US$1.5–1.8bn (HUF350–400bn) in 2009 and US$4bn (HUF900bn) in 2010
	May 2009	#9 US$942mn (HUF 20bn)	US$942mn (HUF 20bn) EU money was allocated to implement the 4 + 1 formula (four days of work and one day of training in a week) to save about 50,000 jobs
	October 28, 2009	#8	Hungary received US$25.1bn from the IMF, EU, and the World Bank
		US$25.1bn	The package consisted of US$15.7bn (€12.5bn) supported by IMF, EU and the World Bank provided a loan of US$8.1bn (€6.5bn) and US$1.3bn (€1.0bn), respectively. The facilities expired in early 2010

(continued)

(continued)

Country	Date	Amount	Item and remarks
	Second half of 2010	#9	The government also launched a special program of US$9.1bn (HUF 1,800 bn, 6.5% of GDP) to support the construction industry for 600 important investment projects to be spread over several years
		US$9.1bn (HUF 1,800 bn, 6.5% of GDP)	
Poland	November 30, 2008	#10 #11	The stimulus package included the "Stability and Development Plan" (SDP) to ensure liquidity of the financial sector, with 45% of the SDP's volume devoted to bank guarantees
		US$31.4bn (PLN91.3bn)	Another US$5.6bn (PLN16.8bn) was allocated to advance investments, co-financed from EU funds (Structural Funds and Cohesion Funds). In addition, US$503mn (PLN1.5bn) were earmarked for supporting renewable energy investments
			The SDP listed not only spending measures, but also two instances of tax increases of US$369mn (PLN1.1bn) from a rise in excise taxes on alcohol and a special tax on cars with engines above 2,000 cm
	January 27, 2009	#12	Polish state-owned bank unlocked US$6bn (PLN20bn) in extra loans for businesses
		US$6bn (PLN20bn) US$131,530 (€100,000)—EU funds	The front-leading of EU funds for infrastructure investments; and a doubling to US$131,530 (€100,000) of the ceiling for tax deductible investments for companies with annual turnover of up to US$1.4mn (€1.2mn) and for newly established firms
			Special Economic Zones were set up to facilitate investments by companies from the automotive, aviation, electronics, machinery, biotech, and renewable energy equipment sectors
	May 2009	#6	
		1. US$27.6 (PLN91.3bn, 0.072% of 2008 GDP)	1. Infrastructure
		2. US$5.1bn (PLN16.8bn, 0.013% of 2008 GDP)	2. Science, R&D, and innovation
		3. US$0.8bn (PLN2.5bn, 0.002% of 2008 GDP)	3. Green technology
	July 30, 2009	#13	Companies experienced orders reduction by at least 25 % year-over-year for three consecutive months between July 2008 and June 2009 gained the opportunity to send employees on a special state-subsidized temporary paid leave for up to 6 months, with government financed about 50 % of the minimum wage
	2008–2010	#6, #14	Including fiscal package—US$5,145mn
		Stimulus package–1.3 % of 2008 GDP	
Romania	November 19, 2008	#15	Romania's government approved a plan to invest more than US$12.6bn (€10bn) between 2009 and 2012 to stimulate growth and create jobs
		US$12.6bn (€10bn)	The Romanian government suspended a tax on new cars to protect jobs in the auto industry

(continued)

(continued)

Country	Date	Amount	Item and remarks
	February 2009	#16 US$16.75bn (€13bn)	The government allocated US$16.75bn (€13bn) to counteract the worst effects of the crisis, which earmarked more than US$12.9bn (€10bn) for infrastructure projects
	March 25, 2009	#17 US$27.1bn (€20bn)	Romania had a 2-year total loan of US$27.1 billion (€20bn) with IMF, EU, EBRD (European Bank for Reconstruction and Development) and World Bank, under the conditions of reducing the budget deficit and freezing wages in the public sector

#1. Dnevnik.bg (January 26, 2009) Bulgarian Government's economy stimulus plan to stay unchanged ahead of 2009 elections, The Sofia Echo. Retrieved from http://sofiaecho.com/2009/01/26/666220_bulgarian-governments-economy-stimulus-plan-to-stay-unchanged-ahead-of-2009-elections
#2. Clarkson, P. (June 29, 2009) Bulgaria provides stimulus package, Glob Maritime. Retrieved from http://www.globmaritime.com/news/rules-regulations/1068-south-american-smash-and-grab.html
#3. Czech Export Bank (November 10, 2008) Topolánek: The Czech Republic has so far fared well through the financial crisis. Retrieved from http://www.ceb.cz/content/view/1134/95/
#4. Dow Jones (February 16, 2009) Czech government approves fiscal stimulus package, tax cuts, FXstreet.com. Retrieved from http://www.fxstreet.com/news/forex-news/article.aspx?storyid=dc5451fe-ece0-4f62-bf70-54f5cdeac0af
#5. Reuters (April 8, 2009) Czech parties agree economic stimulus package, Forex News. Retrieved from http://www.forexpros.com/news/forex-news/update-1-czech-parties-agree-economic-stimulus-package-43355
#6. MTI Econews (November 13, 2008) Hungarian economy minister announces Ft 1.4 trillion stimulus package, Realdeal.hu. Retrieved from http://www.realdeal.hu/20081113/hungarian-economy-minister-announces-ft-14-trillion-stimulus-package/
#7. Békés, G. (October, 2009) Country report Hungary: Economic and political challenges of acceding to the Euro area in the post-Lehaman brothers' world, European Policies Initiative. Retrieved from http://eupi.osi.bg/fce/001/0066/files/HungaryReport.pdf
#8. OECD (June, 2009) *Policy Responses to the Economic Crisis: Investing in innovation for long-term growth*. Retrieved from http://www.oecd.org/dataoecd/59/45/42983414.pdf
#9. Inotai, A. (2010) Hungary Country Report, in: Bertelsmann Stiftung (ed.), *Managing the Crisis. A Comparative Assessment of Economic Governance in 14 Economies*. Gütersloh: Bertelsmann Stiftung. Retrieved from http://www.bertelsmann-transformation-index.de/pdf/Hungary.pdf
#10. Meyer-Ohlendorf, N., Görlach, B., Umpfenbach, K., and Mehling, M. (June, 2009) Economic stimulus in Europe—Accelerating progress towards sustainable development? Ecologic Institute, ESDN Meeting, Prague. Retrieved from http://ecologic.eu/download/projekte/200-249/221-09/ESDN_Recovery_Report.pdf
#11. BBC (December 1, 2008) Poland launches stimulus package. Retrieved from http://news.bbc.co.uk/2/hi/business/7758154.stm
#12. PMR (January 29, 2009a) Government increases stimulus package, admits growth could be slower. Retrieved from http://www.polishmarket.com/68756/Government-increases-stimulus-package-admits-growth-could-be-slower.shtml
#13. PMR (July 31, 2009b) President signs off on job protection package. Retrieved from http://www.polishmarket.com/74391/President-signs-off-on-job-protection-package.shtml
#14. Breuss, F., Kaniovski, S., and Schratzenstaller, M. (2009) Macro-economic Effects of the Fiscal Stimulus Measures in Austria. *Austrian Economic Quarterly* (14.4) pp. 205-216. Retrieved from http://fritz.breuss.wifo.ac.at/Breuss_Kaniovski_Schratzenstaller_Macro-economic_Effects_Fiscal_Stimulus_Austria_AEQ_4_2009.PDF
#15. M.D.P. (November 20, 2008) Romanian cabinet approves EU10 billion stimulus plan, Romania Factor. Retrieved from http://romania-factor.blogspot.com/2008/11/romanian-cabinet-approves-eu10-billion.html
#16. Admin (n.d.) EBRD criticizes Romania for 'imaginary' crisis stimulus package, Business Review. Retrieved from http://business-review.ro/pthe-stimulus-the-romanian-government-intended-to-revive-the-countryrsquos-economy-ldquohas-been-more-imaginary-than-realrdquo-according-to-a-report-from-the-european-bank-f/
#17. Zaman, G. and Georgescu, G. (2009) The impact of global crisis on Romania's economic development. *Annales Universitatis Apulensis Series Oeconomica*, 11(2), pp. 611–124. Retrieved from http://www.oeconomica.uab.ro/upload/lucrari/1120092/01.pdf

Appendix 2
Important Meetings Held by World Leaders to Address the 2008 Global Financial Crisis

Date	Place	Participants
June 18–19, 2012	Los Cabos, Mexico	G20
June 17, 2012	Los Cabos, Mexico	G7 finance ministers
March 1–2, 2012	Brussels	European Council
January 30, 2012	Brussels	Informal meeting of members of the European Council
December 8–9, 2011	Brussels	European Council
November 12–13, 2011	Honolulu, USA	19th APEC Economic Leaders' meeting
November 3–4, 2011	Cannes, France	G20
October 23, 2011	Brussels	European Council
September 10, 2011	Marseille	G8 Deauville Partnership finance ministers
September 9–10, 2011	Marseille	G7 finance ministers and central bank governors
July 21, 2011	Brussels	Meeting of heads of state or government of the Euro area
June 23–24, 2011	Brussels	European Council
March 24–25, 2011	Brussels	European Council
March 17, 2011	Japan	G7 finance ministers telephone conference
March 11, 2011	Brussels	Extraordinary European Council
February 4, 2011	Brussels	European Council
December 16-17, 2010	Brussels	European Council
November 21, 2010	Ireland	G7 finance ministers
November 13–14, 2010	Yokohama, Japan	18th APEC Economic Leaders' Meeting
November 11–12, 2010	Seoul, Korea	G20
October 28–29, 2010	Brussels	European Council
October 8, 2010	Washington DC	G7 finance ministers and central bank governors
September 16, 2010	Brussels	European Council
June 26–27, 2010	Toronto, Canada	G20
June 17, 2010	Brussels	European Council
March 25–26, 2010	Brussels	European Council

(continued)

C. Y.-Y. Lin et al., *National Intellectual Capital and the Financial Crisis in Bulgaria, Czech Republic, Hungary, Romania, and Poland*, SpringerBriefs in Economics,
DOI: 10.1007/978-1-4614-8018-1, © The Author(s) 2014

(continued)

Date	Place	Participants
February 11, 2010	Brussels	Informal meeting of heads of state or government of the European Union
February 5–6, 2010	Iqaluit, Nunavut, Canada	G7 finance ministers and central bank governors
December 10–11, 2009	Brussels	European Council
November 19, 2009	Brussels	Informal meeting of heads of state or government of the European Union
November 14–15, 2009	Singapore	17th APEC Economic Leaders' Meeting
October 29–30, 2009	Brussels	European Council
October 3, 2009	Istanbul, Turkey	G7 finance ministers and central bank governors
September 24–25, 2009	Pittsburgh, USA	G20
September 17, 2009	Brussels	Informal meeting of heads of state or government of the European Union
June 18-19, 2009	Brussels	European Council
June 12-13, 2009	Lecce, Italy	G8 finance ministers
April 24, 2009	Washington DC	G7 finance ministers and central bank governors
April 2, 2009	G20 London Summit, United Kingdom	G20
March 19–20, 2009	Brussels	European Council
February 2009	Rome	G7 finance ministers and central bank governors
December 11–12, 2008	Brussels	European Council
November 2008	Peru	G20 APEC
November 22–23, 2008	Lima, Peru	16th APEC Economic Leaders' Meeting
November 14–15, 2008	Washington D.C., USA	G7
October 15–16, 2008	Brussels	European Council
October 10, 2008	Washington, DC	G7 Finance ministers
September 1, 2008	Brussels	Extraordinary European Council
July 7–9, 2008	Tokyo, Japan	34th G8 Summit
June 19–20, 2008	Brussels	European Council
June 13–14, 2008	Osaka	G8 finance ministers meeting
March 13–14, 2008	Brussels	European Council
February 9, 2008	Tokyo	G7 finance ministers and central bank governors meeting

For further information
http://g20mexico.org/en/g20/previous-leaders-summits
http://www.g8.utoronto.ca/finance/index.htm
http://video.consilium.europa.eu/ecofin/
http://www.european-council.europa.eu/council-meetings/conclusions
http://www.apec.org/

Appendix 3
Indicators in Each Type of Capital

Human capital index	Market capital index
1. Skilled labor*	1. Corporate tax*
2. Employee training*	2. Cross-border venture*
3. Literacy rate	3. Openness of culture*
4. Higher education enrollment	4. Globalization*
5. Pupil-teacher ratio	5. Transparency*
6. Internet subscribers	6. Image of country*
7. Public expenditure on education	7. Exports of goods
Process capital index	*Renewal capital index*
1. Business competition environment*	1. Business R&D spending
2. Government efficiency*	2. Basic research*
3. Intellectual property rights protection*	3. R&D spending/GDP
4. Capital availability*	4. R&D researchers
5. Computers in use per capita	5. Cooperation between universities and enterprises*
6. Convenience of establishing new firms*	6. Scientific articles
7. Mobile phone subscribers	1. Patents per capita (USPTO + EPO)

Remarks
1. Financial capital is the logarithm of GDP per capita adjusted by purchasing power parity.
2. Indicators marked with an asterisk are rated qualitatively using a scale of 1–10.
3. Indicators with objective numbers are transformed to 1-10 scores, by calculating the ratio to the highest number in that indicator and then multiplying by 10.
4. Readers can refer to the book *National Intellectual Capital: A Comparison of 40 Countries* for model validation details (www.nic40.org)

C. Y.-Y. Lin et al., *National Intellectual Capital and the Financial Crisis in Bulgaria, Czech Republic, Hungary, Romania, and Poland*, SpringerBriefs in Economics,
DOI: 10.1007/978-1-4614-8018-1, © The Author(s) 2014

Appendix 4
Definition of the 29 Indicators

Indicators	Definition
Human capital	
Skilled labor*	Whether skilled labor is readily available
Employee training*	Whether employee training is a high propriety in companies
Literacy rate	Adult (over 15 years) literacy rate as a percentage of population
Higher education enrollment	Percentage of population that has attained at least tertiary education
Pupil-teacher ratio	Ratio of teaching staff to students
Internet subscribers	Number of internet users per 1000 people
Public expenditure on education	Total public expenditure on education (percentage of GDP)
Market capital	
Corporate tax encouragement*	Whether corporate taxes encourage entrepreneurial activity
Cross-border venture*	Whether international transactions can be freely negotiated with foreign partners
Openness to foreign culture*	Whether the national culture is open to foreign culture ideas
Attitudes toward globalization*	Whether attitudes toward globalization are generally positive in a given society
Transparency*	Whether transparency of government policy is satisfactory
Country image*	Whether the image abroad of a given country encourages business development
Exports of goods	Exports of goods (Percentage of GDP)
Process capital	
Business competition environment*	Whether competition legislation is efficient in preventing unfair competition
Government efficiency*	Whether government bureaucracy hinders business activity
Intellectual property rights protection*	Whether intellectual property rights are adequately enforced

(continued)

C. Y.-Y. Lin et al., *National Intellectual Capital and the Financial Crisis in Bulgaria, Czech Republic, Hungary, Romania, and Poland*, SpringerBriefs in Economics,
DOI: 10.1007/978-1-4614-8018-1, © The Author(s) 2014

(continued)

Indicators	Definition
Capital availability*	Whether cost of capital encourages business development
Computers in use per capita	Number of computers per 1000 people
Convenience of establishing new firms*	Whether creation of firms is supported by legislation
Mobile phone subscribers	Number of subscribers per 1000 inhabitants
Renewal capital	
Business R&D spending	Business expenditure on R&D (per capita)
Basic research*	Whether basic research enhances long-term economic development
R&D spending/GDP	Total expenditure on R&D (percentage of GDP)
R&D researchers	Total R&D personnel nationwide per capita (Full-time work equivalent per 1000 people)
Cooperation between universities and enterprises*	Whether knowledge transfer is highly developed between universities and companies
Scientific articles	Scientific articles published by origin of author (per capita)
Patents per capita (USPTO + EPO)	USPTO and EPO total patents granted (per capita)
Financial capital	
GDP per capita (PPP) (From IMF)	Gross domestic product based on purchasing-power-parity (PPP) per capita

Remark
Indicators marked with an asterisk are rated qualitatively using a scale of 1–10.

Appendix 5
48 Countries by Cluster and by Continent

This booklet series covers a total of 48 countries in 11 country clusters. China, Brazil, and South Africa are grouped twice to maintain cluster completeness. China is in both Greater China region and BRICKS region, Brazil is in both BRICKS region and Latin American region, and South Africa is in both BRICKS region and in Cluster 5.

Eleven country clusters:

1. Portugal, Italy, Greece, Spain
2. Greater China region (China, Hong Kong, Singapore, Taiwan)
3. Brazil, Russia, India, China, Korea, South Africa (BRICKS)
4. Indonesia, Malaysia, the Philippines, Thailand
5. Israel, Jordan, Turkey, South Africa
6. Bulgaria, Czech Republic, Hungary, Romania, Poland
7. Austria, Belgium, the Netherlands, Switzerland
8. France, Germany, Ireland, United Kingdom
9. Argentina, Brazil, Chile, Colombia, Mexico, Venezuela
10. Australia, Canada, Japan, New Zealand, USA
11. Denmark, Finland, Iceland, Norway, Sweden

48 countries by continent:
Europe—24 countries
Nordic Europe—Denmark, Finland, Iceland, Norway, and Sweden,
Western Europe—Austria, Belgium, France, Germany, Ireland, Netherlands, Switzerland, and UK.
Southern Europe—Greece, Italy, Portugal, and Spain
Eastern Europe—Russia
East Central Europe—Bulgaria, Czech Republic, Hungary, Poland, Romania, and Turkey
Americas—8 countries
North America—Canada, USA
Latin America—Argentina, Brazil, Chile, Colombia, Mexico, and Venezuela
Australia—2 countries
Australia and New Zealand

C. Y.-Y. Lin et al., *National Intellectual Capital and the Financial Crisis in Bulgaria, Czech Republic, Hungary, Romania, and Poland*, SpringerBriefs in Economics,
DOI: 10.1007/978-1-4614-8018-1, © The Author(s) 2014

Asia—13 countries

East Asia—China, Hong Kong, Japan, Korea, and Taiwan

West Asia—Israel, Jordan

Southeast Asia—Indonesia, Malaysia, Philippines, Singapore, and Thailand

South Asia—India

Africa—1 country

South Africa

Appendix 6
National Intellectual Capital Scores and Ranking for 48 Countries (2005–2010)

C. Y.-Y. Lin et al., *National Intellectual Capital and the Financial Crisis in Bulgaria, Czech Republic, Hungary, Romania, and Poland*, SpringerBriefs in Economics,
DOI: 10.1007/978-1-4614-8018-1, © The Author(s) 2014

2005–2010	Human capital		Market capital		Process capital		Renewal capital		Financial capital		NIC	
Mean	6.420		5.409		5.345		3.658		9.115		29.946	
SD	1.217		1.085		1.454		2.056		0.690		5.840	
Country	Score	Ranking	Score	Ranking	Score	Ranking	Score	Ranking	Score	Ranking	Score	Ranking
Argentina	5.370	36	3.340	47	3.038	47	1.413	45	8.755	34	21.916	45
Australia	7.205	15	6.199	12	6.938	9	4.927	16	9.695	11	34.964	13
Austria	7.229	14	6.203	11	6.982	8	5.296	12	9.708	10	35.418	11
Belgium	7.666	8	5.519	23	5.924	21	4.706	17	9.635	14	33.450	19
Brazil	4.757	44	4.589	38	3.076	46	1.753	36	8.481	40	22.656	42
Bulgaria	5.493	34	4.929	31	4.054	36	1.589	41	8.646	37	24.710	35
Canada	7.855	6	6.137	13	6.464	15	5.064	14	9.710	9	35.229	12
Chile	5.414	35	6.663	5	5.163	28	1.710	37	8.784	32	27.734	30
China	4.942	39	5.184	28	3.746	40	2.099	33	7.967	44	23.938	40
Colombia	4.941	40	4.677	36	3.951	37	1.435	44	8.348	42	23.352	41
Czech Republic	5.995	30	5.720	18	5.378	25	2.905	24	9.271	27	29.269	25
Denmark	8.545	1	6.662	6	7.642	1	6.587	6	9.665	13	39.101	3
Finland	7.601	9	6.232	10	7.399	3	7.755	3	9.606	17	38.593	4
France	6.956	20	4.141	45	5.730	22	4.500	20	9.585	18	30.912	23
Germany	6.761	23	5.630	19	6.489	14	5.796	9	9.612	16	34.287	17
Greece	5.986	31	4.216	43	4.113	35	2.168	32	9.440	23	25.923	31
Hong Kong	6.564	25	8.090	2	7.209	5	3.277	23	9.794	4	34.934	14
Hungary	6.674	24	4.836	32	5.095	29	2.301	29	9.046	29	27.952	29
Iceland	8.357	3	5.614	21	6.561	12	5.931	8	9.713	8	36.154	8
India	3.926	48	5.620	20	3.556	42	1.954	34	7.285	48	22.340	44
Indonesia	4.062	47	4.832	33	3.257	44	1.519	42	7.594	46	21.263	47
Ireland	7.145	16	6.816	3	6.711	11	4.101	21	9.768	5	34.541	16

(continued)

(continued)

2005–2010	Human capital		Market capital		Process capital		Renewal capital		Financial capital		NIC	
Mean	6.420		5.409		5.345		3.658		9.115		29.946	
SD	1.217		1.085		1.454		2.056		0.690		5.840	
Country	Score	Ranking	Score	Ranking	Score	Ranking	Score	Ranking	Score	Ranking	Score	Ranking
Israel	8.040	4	5.954	16	6.454	17	7.091	4	9.414	24	36.953	6
Italy	6.471	28	4.155	44	5.184	27	2.745	26	9.479	22	28.035	28
Japan	7.581	10	4.820	34	6.209	18	6.473	7	9.576	19	34.659	15
Jordan	5.345	37	5.341	26	4.411	32	2.212	30	7.865	45	25.174	33
Korea	6.964	19	5.123	29	5.282	26	4.595	19	9.383	25	31.348	22
Malaysia	6.538	26	6.410	9	5.567	23	2.186	31	8.740	35	29.442	24
Mexico	4.871	42	4.491	39	3.226	45	1.237	48	8.781	33	22.606	43
Netherlands	7.312	12	6.761	4	6.879	10	5.163	13	9.739	7	35.855	10
New Zealand	7.123	18	5.999	15	6.460	16	3.701	22	9.380	26	32.662	21
Norway	7.936	5	6.055	14	7.008	7	4.961	15	9.987	1	35.947	9
Philippines	4.772	43	4.464	40	3.317	43	1.268	47	7.481	47	21.302	46
Poland	6.393	29	4.246	41	3.895	38	1.819	35	8.945	30	25.299	32
Portugal	6.882	22	4.801	35	5.470	24	2.467	27	9.224	28	28.844	26
Romania	5.829	32	4.219	42	3.806	39	1.685	38	8.594	39	24.133	39
Russia	5.530	33	3.860	46	3.588	41	2.349	28	8.822	31	24.150	38
Singapore	7.144	17	8.306	1	7.506	2	5.416	11	9.961	2	38.334	5
South Africa	4.708	45	4.976	30	4.472	31	1.677	39	8.472	41	24.306	37
Spain	6.524	27	4.649	37	5.033	30	2.787	25	9.484	21	28.476	27
Sweden	8.385	2	6.563	7	7.174	6	7.780	2	9.673	12	39.575	1
Switzerland	7.575	11	6.481	8	7.374	4	7.988	1	9.753	6	39.172	2
Taiwan	7.244	13	5.823	17	6.026	20	5.425	10	9.526	20	34.044	18

(continued)

(continued)

2005–2010	Human capital		Market capital		Process capital		Renewal capital		Financial capital		NIC	
Mean	6.420		5.409		5.345		3.658		9.115		29.946	
SD	1.217		1.085		1.454		2.056		0.690		5.840	
Country	Score	Ranking	Score	Ranking	Score	Ranking	Score	Ranking	Score	Ranking	Score	Ranking
Thailand	5.310	38	5.524	22	4.365	33	1.436	43	8.304	43	24.938	34
Turkey	4.703	46	5.227	27	4.167	34	1.666	40	8.690	36	24.453	36
United Kingdom	6.939	21	5.440	24	6.090	19	4.697	18	9.626	15	32.793	20
USA	7.695	7	5.348	25	6.558	13	6.715	5	9.886	3	36.202	7
Venezuela	4.884	41	2.761	48	2.545	48	1.277	46	8.625	38	20.092	48

Appendix 7
Country Profile: Additional Statistics

1. **International Reserves in Millions of US$**

Country	2005	2006	2007	2008	2009	2010
Bulgaria	8,200	7,746	11,112	17,955	14,546	15,072
Czech Republic	27,355	29,489	31,447	37,571	36,481	39,250
Hungary	17,259	21,540	22,568	26,516	36,923	45,430
Poland	36,796	42,327	48,579	73,853	58,200	81,554
Romania	16,112	21,972	28,672	39,798	33,392	44,441

Source: Global Finance http://www.gfmag.com/

2. **GDP per capita—PPP Current international dollar**

Country	2005	2006	2007	2008	2009	2010
Bulgaria	9,941	10,989	12,104	13,192	12,655	12,851
Czech Republic	20,281	22,301	24,279	25,191	24,166	24,869
Hungary	16,939	18,107	18,804	19,413	18,306	18,738
Poland	13,571	14,896	16,383	17,598	18,058	18,936
Romania	9,403	10,493	11,509	12,645	11,881	11,860

Source: World Economic Outlook Database http://www.imf.org/external/ns/cs.aspx?id = 28

3. **GDP (PPP)—share of world total_%**

Country	2005	2006	2007	2008	2009	2010
Bulgaria	0.14	0.14	0.14	0.14	0.14	0.13
Czech Republic	0.37	0.37	0.37	0.37	0.36	0.35
Hungary	0.30	0.30	0.28	0.28	0.26	0.25
Poland	0.91	0.92	0.94	0.96	0.98	0.97
Romania	0.36	0.37	0.37	0.39	0.36	0.34

Source: World Economic Outlook Database http://www.imf.org/external/ns/cs.aspx?id = 28

C. Y.-Y. Lin et al., *National Intellectual Capital and the Financial Crisis in Bulgaria, Czech Republic, Hungary, Romania, and Poland*, SpringerBriefs in Economics,
DOI: 10.1007/978-1-4614-8018-1,

4. **Gross domestic expenditure on R&D as a % of GDP**

Country	2005	2006	2007	2008	2009	2010
Bulgaria	0.50	0.49	0.49	0.48	0.48	0.53
Czech Republic	1.27	1.42	1.54	1.54	1.47	1.53
Hungary	0.88	0.94	1.00	0.97	0.97	1.15
Poland	0.54	0.57	0.56	0.56	0.61	0.67
Romania	0.39	0.39	0.45	0.53	0.58	0.47

Source: IMD World Competitiveness Yearbook 2006–2011

5. **Household saving rates_ Percent of disposable household income**

Country	2005	2006	2007	2008	2009	2010
Bulgaria	-	-	-	-	-	-
Czech Republic	4.8	6.1	5.7	4.8	6.1	5.7
Hungary	6.7	7.2	3.3	2.7	4.5	2.5
Poland	7.3	7.5	6.1	0.8	7.8	9.0
Romania	-	-	-	-	-	-

Source: Global Finance http://www.gfmag.com/

Glossary

Basel II is the second of the Basel Accords, which are recommendations on banking laws and regulations issued by the Basel Committee on Banking Supervision. Basel II, initially published in June 2004, was intended to create an international standard for banking regulators to control how much capital banks need to put aside to guard against the types of financial and operational risks banks face.

BBC British Broadcasting Corporation

CNB Czech National Bank

CIA The USA Central Intelligence Agency

CPI Consumer price inflation

CSD Center for the Study of Democracy

EBRD European Bank for Reconstruction and Development

ECB European Central Bank

EFSF European Financial Stability Facility, scheduled to expire in 2013

ESM European Stabilization Mechanism, a permanent crisis mechanism to replace EFSF

EU European Union

FDI Foreign direct investment

GCI Global Competitiveness Index (published by World Economic Forum)

GDP Gross domestic product

GDP per capita (ppp) Gross domestic product per capita adjusted by purchasing power parity

IMD International Institute for Management Development, Switzerland

C. Y.-Y. Lin et al., *National Intellectual Capital and the Financial Crisis in Bulgaria, Czech Republic, Hungary, Romania, and Poland*, SpringerBriefs in Economics,
DOI: 10.1007/978-1-4614-8018-1,

IMF International Monetary Fund

IP Intellectual Property

Long-term NIC Long-term oriented national intellectual capital, represented by human capital and renewal capital

MDG Millennium Development Goals

New Basel III Maastricht criteria liquidity regulations—There are four main criteria: demonstrated price stability—inflation, sustainable fiscal position (measured both by government deficit and government debt 60% of GDP), exchange rate stability, and convergence in long-term interest rates.

NIC National intellectual capital

OECD Organization for Economic Cooperation and Development

PPP Purchasing power parity

R&D Research and development

RC Renewal capital

RES Renewable energy sources

SDP Stability and Development Plan in Poland

Short-term NIC Short-term oriented national intellectual capital, represented by market capital and process capital

SMEs Small- and Medium-Sized Enterprises

Three time periods For the convenience of comparing ranking changes, the six years data were separated into three time periods, namely 2005–2006, 2007–2008, and 2009–2010. Two years each represents "before, during, and after" the 2008 global financial crisis. Even though Euro zone is still in sovereign debt trouble as of mid-2012, the time partition is based on the financial crisis progression in the epicenter. The signs of financial trouble appeared in 2007 and the crisis was declared over in the third quarter of 2009.

USPTO United States Patent and Trademark Office

VAT Value-added tax

References

Altman RC (2009) The great crash, 2008: a geopolitical setback for the west, foreign affair, the council on Foreign Relations. http://www.foreignaffairs.com/articles/63714/roger-c-altman/the-great-crash-2008. Accessed 2 Jan 2009

Angelov G (2009) Country report Bulgaria: economic and political challenges of acceding to the Euro area in the post-Lehman brothers' world, European policies initiative, open society institute—Sofia. http://eupi.osi.bg/fce/001/0066/files/BulgariaReport.pdf

Ban D (2010) Romania: economic woes deepen, Balcani Caucaso organization. http://www.balcanicaucaso.org/eng/Regions-and-countries/Romania/Romania-Economic-Woes-Deepen. Accessed 19 Mar 2010

Barnes S (2010) OECD economic surveys: Euro Area 2010, resolving and avoiding unsustainable imbalances. Economics department working paper no. 827. DOI: 10.1787/eco_surveys-euz-2010-5-en. http://www.keepeek.com/Digital-Asset-Management/oecd/economics/oecd-economic-surveys-euro-area-2010/resolving-and-avoiding-unsustainable-imbalances_eco_surveys-euz-2010-5-en

Boc E (2011) The reform of the state in Romania (2009–2011). Transylvanian Rev Adm Sci 34E:5–21. http://rtsa.ro/en/files/TRAS-34E-1-BOC.pdf

Bocian M, Sadowski R (2008) Hungary as a victim of the global financial crisis, center of Eastern studies. http://www.osw.waw.pl/en/publikacje/ceweekly/2008-10-23/hungary-victim-global-financial-crisis. Accessed 22 Oct 2008

Bryant L (2011) Growth expected to slow in world's largest economies, voice of America news. http://www.voanews.com/english/news/europe/OECD-Economic-Slowdown-Likely-to-Continue-129458543.html

Center for the Study of Democracy (CSD) (2011) The hidden economy in Bulgaria after the economic crisis, Friedrich Ebert foundation, office of Bulgaria, center for the study of democracy policy brief no. 28. http://library.fes.de/pdf-files/bueros/sofia/08099.pdf

Center for the Study of Democracy (CSD) (n.d.) The informal economy in Bulgaria: policy responses in an economic crisis, center for the study of democracy. http://www.csd.bg/artShow.php?id=9553

Central Intelligence Agency (CIA) (2012) The world factbook, U.S.A. central intelligence agency. https://www.cia.gov/library/publications/the-world-factbook/index.html

Dapontas D (2011) Currency crisis: the case of Hungary (2008-2009) using two stage least squares, special conference paper, bank of Greece, Eurosystem. http://www.bankofgreece.gr/BogEkdoseis/SCP201113.pdf. Accessed Feb 2011

Dietz M, Homonnay A, Shvakman I (2012) What's ahead for banking in Eastern Europe, Mckinsey quarterly. https://www.mckinseyquarterly.com/Financial_Services/Banking/Whats_ahead_for_banking_in_Eastern_Europe_2929

Dikov I (2009) Bulgaria 2008 review: global financial crisis and Bulgaria, Novinite.com Sofia new agency. http://www.novinite.com/view_news.php?id=100148. Accessed 2 Jan 2009

C. Y.-Y. Lin et al., *National Intellectual Capital and the Financial Crisis in Bulgaria, Czech Republic, Hungary, Romania, and Poland*, SpringerBriefs in Economics,
DOI: 10.1007/978-1-4614-8018-1,

Dobrota G (2012) The effects of the world-wide economic and financial crisis on the Romanian economy under the impact of the fiscal policy measures. Econ Financ Rev 1(12):9–18. http://www.businessjournalz.org/articlepdf/EFR_11012mar2012.pdf

Draper P, Freytag A, Voll S (2009) Global financial crisis, protectionism and current account deficit: South Africa on the brink? Working paper no. 8 global financial markets, University Jena and University Halle. http://pubdb.wiwi.uni-jena.de/pdf/wp_hlj08-2009.pdf

Edvinsson L, Malone MS (1997) Intellectual capital: realizing your company's true value by finding its hidden brainpower. HarperBusiness, New York

Ernst, Young (2009) E&Y: FDI stagnates in Europe due to crisis: Czech Republic remains in the top 20, Ernst and Young. http://www.czechinvest.org/en/ey-fdi-stagnates-in-europe-due-to-crisis-czech-republic-remains-in-the-top-20. Accessed 4 June 2009

Ersado L (2009) Bulgaria: poverty implications of the global financial crisis, human development sector unit, ministry of labor and social policy, Europe and central Asia region, the World Bank. http://siteresources.worldbank.org/BULGARIAEXTN/Resources/305438-1224088560466/Bulgaria_The_Global_Financial_Crisis_and_Poverty_Implications_Report.pdf

EU-27 Watch (2012) The effects of financial crisis on Poland, foundation for European studies—European Institute. http://www.eu-27watch.org/?q=node/109. Accessed Jul 2012

Europa (2008) The global financial crisis and its impact on Bulgaria, European commission, economy finance. http://ec.europa.eu/economy_finance/pdf/2008/autumnforecasts/bg_en.pdf

European Economic Advisory Group (EEAG) (2012) The Hungarian crisis, European economic advisory group report on the European economy. CESifo, Munich, pp 115–130. http://www.cesifo-group.de/portal/pls/portal/docs/1/1213659.PDF

European Union (2010) Council opinion on the updated convergence program of Bulgaria, 2009–2012. Official J Eur Union. http://eur-lex.europa.eu/LexUriServ/LexUriServ.do?uri=OJ:C:2010:137:0012:0016:EN:PDF

Fackler M (2008) Financial crisis spreads to emerging nations. The New York Times. http://www.nytimes.com/2008/10/24/business/worldbusiness/24won.html. Accessed 23 Oct 2008

Gheorghiu A, Gheorghiu A (2011) Romania's country risk evolution throughout the years of crisis, Hyperion University, Bucharest, Romania. http://www.wz.uph.edu.pl/zeszyty/archiwalne/91-2011_4.pdf

Global Finance (2012), http://www.gfmag.com

Greenhouse S (1990) Evolution in Europe: east Europe finds pain on journey to capitalism The New York Times. http://www.nytimes.com/1990/11/10/world/evolution-in-europe-east-europe-finds-pain-on-journey-to-capitalism.html?pagewanted=all&src=pm

Gurzo I, Molnar I (2011) Political, economic and social changes in Hungary (2002–2011) problems and progress. Seria Stiinte Economice Anul 21(Partea I):83–88

Harrington C (2011) The Spanish financial crisis. International Finance and Development, University of Iowa. http://blogs.law.uiowa.edu/ebook/content/spanish-financial-crisis

Heritage Foundation (2012) Economic freedom, the Heritage Foundation. http://www.heritage.org. Accessed Jun 2012

Horvath J (2009) 2008 Hungarian financial crisis, Case network E-briefs. http://www.case-research.eu/upload/publikacja_plik/23686666_E-brief_012009%20FINAL.pdf

Hugh E (2012) Hungary economy watch. http://hungaryeconomywatch.blogspot.com/. 12 Jan 2012

Inotai A (2010) Hungary country report. In: Bertelsmann Stiftung (ed) Managing the crisis. A comparative assessment of economic governance in 14 economies. Bertelsmann Stiftung, Gütersloh http://www.bertelsmann-transformation-index.de/pdf/Hungary.pdf

International Monetary Fund (IMF) (2008) Czech Republic—2008 article IV consultation, concluding statement of IMF mission. Int Monetary Fund. http://www.imf.org/external/np/ms/2008/112408a.htm

International Monetary Fund (IMF) (2009) Romania received support from the IMF to counter crisis, Int Monetary Fund. http://www.imf.org/external/pubs/ft/survey/so/2009/int050409a.htm. Accessed 4 May 2009

International Monetary Fund (IMF) (2012a) World economic outlook update: global recovery stalls, downside risks intensify, Int Monetary Fund. http://www.imf.org/external/pubs/ft/weo/2012/update/01/. Accessed 24 Jan 2012

International Monetary Fund (IMF) (2012b) Czech Republic—2012 article IV consultation concluding statement. Int Monetary Fund. http://www.imf.org/external/np/ms/2012/022712.htm. Accessed 27 Feb 2012

International Monetary Fund (IMF) (2012c) IMF Executive Board Concludes 2012 Article IV Consultation with the Czech Republic, Int Monetary Fund. http://www.imf.org/external/np/sec/pn/2012/pn1252.htm. Accessed 18 May 2012

Kattel R (2010) Financial and economic crisis in eastern Europe, network ideas. http://www.networkideas.org/featart/jan2010/Eastern_Europe.pdf

Kehoe T (2010) The current financial crisis in Spain: what should we learn from the great depressions of the twentieth century? University of Minnesota and Federal Reserve Bank of Minneapolis, 18th Barcelona Lecture, Barcelona G.S.E. and Banc Sabadell, Feb 2010

Kluza S (n.d.) The financial crisis: Poland's experience, Polish Financial Supervision Authority. http://siteresources.worldbank.org/FINANCIALSECTOR/Resources/Day1KluzaFinancialCrisisPanelPoland.pdf

Lin CYY (2011) Leveraging intellectual capital for future competitiveness in Finland, Presentation at Tekes, Helsinki, 10 Nov 2011

Lin CYY, Edvinsson L (2011) National intellectual capital: a comparison of 40 countries. Springer, New York

Magas I (2010) Impacts of the financial crisis on a small open economy: the case of Hungary. Int Relat Quart 1(3):1–20

Mendonça JR (2010) The impact of the international financial crisis on Brazil. http://www.realinstitutoelcano.org/wps/portal/rielcano_eng/Content?WCM_GLOBAL_CONTEXT=/elcano/elcano_in/zonas_in/international+economy/ari38-2010

Mihaylova A (2009) Bulgaria adopts anti-crisis measures. Dalje.com Global Crisis. http://dalje.com/en-world/bulgaria-adopts-anti-crisis-measures/276215

Minassian G (2011) Country report: Bulgaria, Institute for Economic Studies, Bulgarian Academy of Sciences. Project LINK Fall meeting, DESA UN, New York, USA. http://projects.chass.utoronto.ca/link/meeting/ctryrep/BGR_201110.pdf

Moloney N (2010) EU financial market regulation after the global financial crisis: "More Europe" or more risks? Common Mark Law Rev 47:1317–1383

Nanto DK (2009) The global financial crisis: analysis and policy implications, CRS report for Congress RL34742, Congr Res Serv. http://www.fas.org/sgp/crs/misc/RL34742.pdf

Nonchev A, Mantcheva D, Vassileva E, Stefanov R, Yalamov T (2011) The hidden economy in Bulgaria and the global economic crisis. Center for the Study of Democracy with the support of Friedrich Ebert Stiftung. ISBN: 989-954-477-181-2

Novinite (2012) IMF's spring outlook slashes Bulgaria's economic growth forecast, Novinite.com, Sofia news agency. http://www.novinite.com/view_news.php?id=138587. Accessed 17 April 2102

OECD (2009) Policy Responses to the economic crisis: investing in innovation for long-term growth. http://www.oecd.org/dataoecd/59/45/42983414.pdf. Accessed Jun 2009

OECD (2010a) Economic survey of Czech Republic 2010: the challenge of fiscal consolidation after the crisis. OECD. http://www.oecd.org/document/44/0,3746,en_33873108_33873293_44875436_1_1_1_1,00.html. Accessed 6 Apr 2010

OECD (2010b) Economic survey of Hungary, 2010. Policy Brief. http://www.oecd.org/dataoecd/58/55/44577243.pdf

OECD (2010c) Economic survey of Poland, 2010. Policy Brief, OECD. http://www.oecd.org/dataoecd/5/28/44904949.pdf

OECD (2012a) Czech Republic—Economic forecast summary (May 2012). OECD. http://www.oecd.org/document/63/0,3746,en_33873108_33873293_45269183_1_1_1_1,00.html

OECD (2012b) Czech Republic, Development in Individual OECD countries. http://www.keepeek.com/Digital-Asset-Management/oecd/economics/oecd-economic-outlook-volume-2012-issue-1/czech-republic_eco_outlook-v2012-1-15-en

OECD (2012c) Economic survey of Hungary 2012. OECD. http://www.oecd.org/document/38/0,3746,en_2649_33733_49830438_1_1_1_1,00.html

OECD (2012d) Economic survey of Poland 2012. OECD. http://www.oecd.org/document/15/0,3746,en_2649_33733_49945551_1_1_1_1,00.html

OECD (2012e) Hungary—Economic forecast summary (May 2012). OECD. http://www.oecd.org/document/55/0,3746,en_33873108_33873438_45269939_1_1_1_1,00.html

Piatkowska A (2010) Poland 2010 report: economy, ministry of economy, analyses and forecasting department. http://www.mg.gov.pl/files/upload/9142/RoG100909eng.pdf

Plociennik S (2012) Sources of stability of the polish economy during the economic crisis, Bertelsmann Stiftung. http://www.bertelsmann-stiftung.de/bst/de/media/xcms_bst_dms_35331_35332_2.pdf

QFinance (2012a) Bulgaria economy—economy and trade, QFinance country profiles. http://www.qfinance.com/country-profiles/bulgaria. Accessed Jun 2012

QFinance (2012b) Romania—economy, QFinance. http://www.qfinance.com/country-profiles/romania. Accessed Jun 2012

Reavis C (2009) The global financial crisis of 2008-2009: the role of greed, fear and oligarchs, MIT Sloan Management Case #09-093, published 22 July 2009

Refdahl T, Karstensen K (2009) Financial and currency crisis in the country of Hungary, Master thesis, Master of Science Finance and Strategic Management, Copenhagen Business School. http://studenttheses.cbs.dk/bitstream/handle/10417/802/thomas_svarre_refdahl_og_kasper_karstensen.pdf?sequence=1

Reichardt A (2011) Poland and the global economic crisis: observations and reflections in the public sector. J Finan Manage Pub Serv 10(1):38–48

Reinhart CM, Rogoff KS (2009) This time is different: eight centuries of financial folly. Princeton University Press, Princeton. ISBN 9780691142166

Reuters (2009) Factbox—Europe's fiscal stimulus plans, Reuters. http://www.reuters.com/article/2009/03/17/eu-summit-stimulus-idUSLH44404720090317. Accessed 17 Mar 2009

Reuters (2012) Hungary clears way to IMF talks with central bank law change, Reuters. http://www.reuters.com/article/2012/07/06/us-hungary-imf-idUSBRE8650AU20120706

Rogoff K (2011) In: Javetski B, Koller T Understanding the second great contraction: an interview with Kenneth Rogoff, McKinsey quarterly. https://www.mckinseyquarterly.com/Economic_Studies/Productivity_Performance/Understanding_the_Second_Great_Contraction_An_interview_with_Kenneth_Rogoff_2871

Sbughea C (2011) The origins of the global financial crisis and its impact on Romanian economy, Annals of "Dunarea de Jos" University of Galati, Fascicle I. Econ Appl Inf 17(1):107–112. http://www.ann.ugal.ro/eco/Doc20011_1/Corina_Sbughea.pdf

Schneider O (2009) Country report Czech Republic—economic and political challenges of acceding to the Euro area in the post-Lehman Brothers' world, European Policies Initiative, Open Society Institute—Sofia. http://eupi.osi.bg/fce/001/0066/files/CzechReport.pdf

Schwab K (ed) (2011) The global competitiveness report 2011–2012. World Economic Forum, Geneva

Social Watch (2010) Finance for development in times of crisis, social Watch report 2010, after the fall, national reports. http://www.socialwatch.org/node/12065

Stoilov O (ed) (2009) 2009—the year of the economic crisis, economic Yearbook, Stara Zagora region, 2009, *chamber of commerce and industry—Stara Zagora*. http://www.econsz.com/2009/en/2009-the-year-of-the-economic-crisis

Terazi E, Senel S (2011) The effects of the global financial crisis on the central and eastern European union countries. Int J Bus Soc Sci 2(17):186–192

Valentinyi A (2012) The Hungarian crisis. http://www.voxeu.org/index.php?q=node/7740. Accessed 19 Mar 2012

Valert P (2008) Summary of the Czech Republic rescue plan regarding the financial crisis, DLA Piper. http://www.dlapiper.com/files/upload/%204482139_1_UKGROUPS(EMEA%20Govt%20Rescue%20Plan%20-%20Czech%20Rebublic%20-%2014%20Nov)%20(2).PDF

Voinea L, Pauna B, Lungu L, Cojanu V, Busuioc, A (2010) The 6th GEA report on Romania and the Lisbon Agenda, GDA group of applied economics. http://www.gea.org.ro/documente/en/lisabona/2010/Romania2020.pdf

World Bank (2011) Crisis-proofing financial integration: Czech Republic, World Bank. http://siteresources.worldbank.org/ECAEXT/Resources/258598-1284061150155/7383639-1323888814015/8319788-1324485944855/03_czech.pdf

World Bank (2012) Bulgaria overview, the World Bank. http://www.worldbank.org/en/country/bulgaria/overview

World Bank (n.d.) Managing financial FDIL Poland, World Bank. http://siteresources.worldbank.org/ECAEXT/Resources/258598-1284061150155/7383639-1323888814015/8319788-1324485944855/02_poland.pdf

Zaman G, Georgescu G (2009) The impact of global crisis on Romania's economic development. Annales Universitatis Apulensis Series Oeconomica 11(2):611–124. http://www.oeconomica.uab.ro/upload/lucrari/1120092/01.pdf

Zamfir PB (2010) The global financial crisis, where does place Romanian economy in EU? Annals of the University of Petrosani, Economics 10(1):371–378. http://www.upet.ro/anale/economie/pdf/20100236.pdf

Author Index

C. Y.-Y. Lin et al., *National Intellectual Capital and the Financial Crisis in Bulgaria, Czech Republic, Hungary, Romania, and Poland*, SpringerBriefs in Economics,
DOI: 10.1007/978-1-4614-8018-1, © The Author(s) 2014

Subject Index

C. Y.-Y. Lin et al., *National Intellectual Capital and the Financial Crisis in Bulgaria, Czech Republic, Hungary, Romania, and Poland*, SpringerBriefs in Economics,
DOI: 10.1007/978-1-4614-8018-1,

FSC
www.fsc.org
MIX
Papier | Fördert
gute Waldnutzung
FSC® C083411

Kolibri 360 GmbH
Ferdinand-Jühlke-Straße 7
99095 Erfurt, Deutschland
produktsicherheit@kolibri360.de